Just for Boys!
Reading Comprehension

Grades 6-8

Written by Nat Reed
Illustrated by Amanda Smith, Tom Riddolls

ISBN 978-1-55035-815-5
Copyright 2007
Revised May 2008
All Rights Reserved * Printed in Canada

Published in the United States by:
On The Mark Press
3909 Witmer Road PMB 175
Niagara Falls, New York
14305
www.onthemarkpress.com

Published in Canada by:
S&S Learning Materials
15 Dairy Avenue
Napanee, Ontario
K7R 1M4
www.sslearning.com

At A Glance

Learning Expectations	Grade 6 Fiction	Grade 6 Non-fiction	Grade 7 Fiction	Grade 7 Non-fiction	Grade 8 Fiction	Grade 8 Non-fiction
Vocabulary, Word Usage & Grammar						
• Identify word meanings	•	•	•	•	•	•
• Antonyms / synonyms / idioms	•	•	•		•	•
• Dictionary and thesaurus skills		•				
• Writing complete sentences	•	•	•	•	•	•
Reading Comprehension						
• Identify and describe main text elements	•	•	•	•	•	•
• Understand words in context	•	•	•	•	•	•
• Summarize main elements and provide supporting details	•	•	•	•	•	•
• Identify and describe character traits and relationships between characters	•	•	•	•	•	•
Reasoning and Critical Thinking						
• Analyze and evaluate text elements	•	•	•	•	•	•
• Point of view of a character / person	•	•	•	•	•	•
• Compare and contrast setting or characters / person	•	•	•	•	•	•
• Analyze character / people traits and behaviors	•	•	•	•	•	•
• Identify and describe cause & effect	•	•	•	•	•	•
• Express opinions, provide evidence from text	•	•	•	•	•	•
• Evaluate evidence	•	•	•	•	•	•
• Relate text to one's own experience	•	•	•	•	•	•
• Research skills	•	•	•		•	•
• Make predictions	•	•	•	•	•	•

Table of Contents

Teacher Assessment Rubric

Student's Name: _____

Criteria	Level 1	Level 2	Level 3	Level 4
Comprehension	Responses demonstrate a limited understanding of important information in the passage.	Responses demonstrate a basic understanding of important information in the passage.	Responses demonstrate a good understanding of important information in the passage.	Responses demonstrate a thorough understanding of important information in the passage.
Oral reading	Reads aloud word by word.	May ignore punctuation when reading aloud.	Reads at varying rates depending on purpose and encouragement.	Reads aloud fluently and effortlessly.
Ability to summarize what has been read	Limited summarization of events, main characters, and setting.	Summarizes most of the events, most of the main characters, and setting.	Summarizes the main events, main characters, and setting, with good accuracy.	Accurately and completely summarizes the main events in correct sequence, the main characters, and setting.
Reasoning	Seldom makes sound judgements and draws effective conclusions from materials.	Inconsistent in making sound judgements and drawing effective conclusions from material.	Fairly consistent in making sound judgements and drawing effective conclusions from material.	Consistently makes sound judgements and draws effective conclusions from material.
Understanding form and style	Limited identification of various forms of writing (i.e., poetry, short story, newspaper article) and describing their key features.	Fair success at identification of various forms of writing (i.e., poetry, short story, newspaper article) and describing their key features.	Good identification of various forms of writing (i.e., poetry, short story, newspaper article) and describing their key features.	Demonstrates thorough understanding of various forms of writing (i.e., poetry, short story, newspaper article) and their key features.
Extending beyond text	Responses do not make limited extensions beyond text to other texts and relevant personal experiences.	Responses demonstrate a little extension beyond text, but references are general rather than specific.	Responses demonstrate good extension beyond text to both texts and personal experiences.	Responses demonstrate considerable evidence of extension beyond text to other texts and personal experiences.

Student Self-Assessment Rubric

Name: _____

Put a check mark in the box that best describes your performance. Then, add your points to determine your total score.

Expectations	My Performance				
	Always (4 point)	Frequently (3 points)	Sometimes (2 points)	Needs Improvement (1 point)	My Points
✓ I was focused and stayed on task.					
✓ My answers were thoughtful and showed consistent effort.					
✓ I checked meanings of difficult words/ideas.					
✓ I used all the resources available to me to answer questions.					
✓ I used correct punctuation and sentence structure in my writing.					
✓ I proofread my work for spelling, grammar, and clarity.					
✓ I included my own experiences in my responses whenever possible.					
✓ I know what I do well.					
✓ I know what I need to improve.					

Total Points: _____

Read Aloud Observation Form

Student's Name: _____

This evaluation tool is intended for teacher to use one-on-one with students to assess reading strengths and difficulties. Reading fluency is one of the literacy skills needed for comprehension.

Observation Criteria	Too fast	Too slow	Appropriate
Pace of Reading			

Observation Criteria	Several major mistakes/omissions	Several minor mistakes/omissions	Few mistakes/omissions
Accuracy			

Observable Pattern: _____

Observation Criteria	No expression	Little expression	Appropriate expression
Expression			

Observation Criteria	Few pauses for periods/commas	Some pausing for periods/commas	Consistent pausing for periods/commas
Attention to Punctuation			

Observation Criteria	Few strategies to attack new words	Some strategies to attack new words	Several strategies to attack new words
Decoding			

Strategies Used: _____

Teacher Suggestions

This resource can be used in a variety of ways:

1. The student booklet focuses on a variety of fiction and non-fiction passages. Each of these sections contains the following activities:

    a) Before you read the passages (reasoning and critical thinking skills; dictionary and thesaurus skills);
    b) While you read the passage (comprehension and higher-thinking questions);
    c) After you read the passage (reading comprehension skills; extension activities).

2. Students may read the passage at their own speed and then select, or be assigned, a variety of questions and activities.

3. Bulletin Board and Interest Center Ideas: Themes might include snowboarding, airport security, summer jobs, science fiction, 9/11, true friendship, poetry, high-tech gadgets, and natural disasters.

4. Pre-Reading Activities: This unit may also be used is conjunction with the themes of self-esteem, heroes/courage, the elderly, the homeless, mountain-climbing, smoking, transportation (e.g., bicycles, space ships), holidays (e.g., Halloween and Christmas), sex education, giving a speech, and the wilderness.

5. Independent Reading Approach: Students who are able to work independently may attempt to complete the assignments in a self-directed manner. Initially these students should participate in the pre-reading activities with the rest of the class. Students should familiarize themselves with the reproducible student booklet. Completed worksheets should be submitted so that the teacher can note how quickly and accurately the students are working. Students may be brought together periodically to discuss issues introduced in a specific reading passage.

6. Fine Art Activities: Students may integrate such topics as Christmas and Halloween (cards, decorations, etc.), map-making, designing a poster advertising a summer job, designing their own snowboard or GT, creating an advertisement to persuade other boys from starting to smoke.

7. Encourage the students to keep a reading log in which they record their reading each day and their thoughts about the passages.

Name: _____

LOST!

1. If you were in an unfamiliar forest, how might you avoid getting lost? (Two suggestions)

2. Other than getting lost, what other dangers are present in a forest?

3. How might you go about finding someone who is lost in a forest? (At least one strategy)

4. If you were going for a hike in a forest, what are three survival items you would be sure to take with you?

5. Choose a word from the word bank to complete each definition.

| overcast | prospector | tormentor | landmark | exhausted |

a) Someone who annoys you is a ._____
b) Someone who is very tired is said to be _____
c) A person who searches for gold and other precious metals is a _____
d) A cloudy sky is an _____ sky.
e) A feature such as a hill or large tree is called a _____

LOST!

S eth Jansen stopped under a large poplar tree and glanced up at the sun. It was now hanging just above the treetops on the western horizon. He checked his watch and took a deep breath – 3:20 p.m. For several hours now he'd been going around in circles, trying desperately to find his way back to his uncle's cabin. He took his axe and slashed a piece of bark from the poplar. If nothing else, these markers might help his uncle track him down – if that was even possible now!

How had he ever gotten himself into such a mess – getting lost in one of the world's largest, most remote forests? Just three weeks ago he'd boarded the train to spend the summer in Minnesota's Lake of the Woods with his prospector uncle, Ted . . . and things had been going great too, that is until this morning, when his uncle had hiked over to Nelson Cheechoo's to borrow a chain saw. As soon as Seth had finished his chores, he grabbed an axe and headed into the forest to cut some firewood. Chopping wood was something he really enjoyed – but the morning had been heavily overcast, and before he knew it, Seth was lost. He needed a landmark – something he could use to recover his bearings – a river or high hill. But there was nothing – only bush, trees and rocks . . . Walking toward the sun would

> What might Seth do at this point?

eliminate the danger of going in circles, but for a good part of the afternoon the sky had been cloudy, and he suspected that he'd been going further and further from his uncle's cabin. But he had to do something. He couldn't just sit down under a tree and give up.

 # LOST!

After wandering around for some time, Seth stopped for another rest by a mangled old jack pine and slashed off a chunk of bark at about eye-level. He could see that there was a rise in the terrain before him – a hill. Great! High ground would mean dry walking for the next while. He peered through the brush ahead of them. Maybe at the top of the hill he'd be able to climb a tree and see if he could spot his uncle's cabin – a curl of smoke, anything that would help him find his way.

He found it increasingly difficult to keep panic from edging into his thoughts. Think of something else. The folks back home. His friends at school. The guys on the ball team.

As he reached the crest of the hill, the bush gradually thinned. He stopped, his breathing raspy with exhaustion, his legs almost shaking. It had been almost five hours since he'd left his uncle's cabin and he was starved – he hadn't had anything to eat since breakfast.

One good thing – Uncle Ted would be back from Nelson Cheechoo's by now and was probably out looking for him. Surely when his uncle saw the axe missing, he'd put two and two together. As good a woodsman as his uncle was, though, it would probably be impossible to track Seth down – especially the way he'd been going around in circles.

He sagged to the ground and watched the sun dip below the trees. Soon it would be dark. Something brushed against his arm. Mosquitoes! With dusk coming those tiny tormentors would appear in earnest – not to mention the blackflies . . . He shuddered at the thought.

He took a deep breath and struggled to his feet. He had to get going – stay moving. That was the only way his uncle would ever find him. Yet for some reason Seth suddenly knew that moving on was just the thing he shouldn't do – that he should stay right there under the big black spruce and wait.

The mosquitoes were now out in droves, great swarms buzzing around his face and neck. Then came the blackflies, and finally the tiny, almost invisible sandflies, making their torturous descent on his bare arms and ankles.

> Suggest one strategy that Seth might use to escape harm from the wolves.

An hour passed . . . He was just getting back to his feet to stretch his legs when he heard it – a blood-curdling sound that froze everything inside him.

Wolves! His uncle had warned him about timber wolves, pointing out some of their tracks near the cabin. Wolves!

 LOST!

Again a long, mournful howl drifted toward him on the late afternoon breeze – wafting up from somewhere over to the east – away from the setting sun. Heart pounding, he looked up into the branches of the spruce tree towering above him. He'd be safe up there. Catching the thick branch just above his head he swung himself upward, quickly scrambling from branch to branch until he was about twenty feet above the forest floor.

Another long, wavering howl sent a chill up his spine. They were definitely on his trail and closing in fast! How long would the wolves keep him up here? Until morning? But could he hold on for that long?

From a cluster of trees to his right there was a fleeting movement – then a large dark object flashed into the clearing, howling loudly. They were here!

Seth strained for a better look. How many were there? He remembered his uncle telling him that wolves always ran in packs.

Through the branches of the spruce he could now see something moving about immediately below him. His heart in his mouth, he leaned forward for a better look. There – only a few feet beneath him – its front paws leaning up against the spruce – its great head looking straight up at him – was the largest hound dog Seth had ever seen!

A dog? What on earth would a dog be doing a way out here in the middle of nowhere?

Then he heard the sound of a voice. He could scarcely believe it, for in the next instant he found himself gazing down into the relieved face of his Uncle Ted.

"What are you doing up there, Seth?" his uncle asked. "Picking spruce cones?"

Sheepishly Seth climbed down. "I thought it was a wolf."

When he reached the bottom of the tree, his uncle patted him good-naturedly on the shoulder. "When I got back from Nelson Cheechoo's I waited around for you for an hour or so, then I went back to Nelson's and borrowed old Buster here." He pointed a thumb at the panting hound, now lying in an exhausted heap under the tree. "You were going in so many circles that you made old Buster here dizzier than a sandfly in a windstorm."

"For some reason I felt that I shouldn't move from this old spruce tree."

Uncle Ted nodded. "When we're lost, the worst thing we can do is wander around aimlessly, because when we do, we generally wander further and further from where we should be going. If you'd kept going, goodness knows what might have happened. McGuire's Swamp is on the other side of this hill. I don't think even old Buster could track someone through that."

"I guess there's still a lot I need to learn about living in the woods," Seth said with a grin.

"Now come on, nephew," his uncle said, smiling broadly. "There's a big moose steak waiting back at the cabin for this old hound dog. Let's get home."

Name: _____

LOST!

1. Why had Seth gone into the forest after finishing his chores?

2. How did the weather contribute to Seth getting lost?

3. Why was Seth slashing bark from trees along the way?

4. Why do you think people who are lost often end up going in circles?

5. Why did Seth climb the tree?

6. If you were Uncle Ted, would you be upset with Seth? Why or why not?

7. Where did Uncle Ted get Buster? Why did he get him?

Name: _____

Crazy Legs

1. Think back to when you were seven or eight years old. What were some of your favorite things to do during this time of your life? What was there about these activities that made them so enjoyable?

2. Do you know anyone who is a little "different" in the way they dress, speak or act? Describe how such a person may be viewed by others in the community. Why do you think people might feel this way?

3. In this story, one of the characters is an older man who loves to ride around town on his bike. Why might this behavior seem odd to some people?

4. Many adults, both male and female, enjoy writing poetry. What topics do you think men would enjoy writing poems about? (Try to think of three examples.)

5. Antonyms are words with opposite meanings. Draw a line from each word in column A to its antonym in column B.

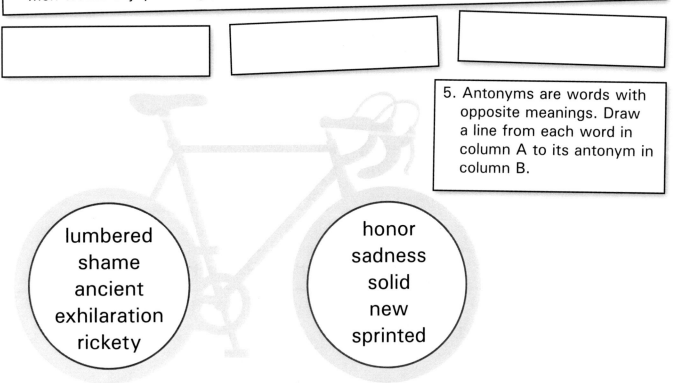

lumbered
shame
ancient
exhilaration
rickety

honor
sadness
solid
new
sprinted

Crazy Legs

D ave Engel shuddered as he trailed his uncle up a set of rickety stairs into a stale-smelling room on the second floor. "Who owned this place before you, Jake?"
"Old Man Henderson. He was that funny character who rode around town on his bicycle all the time."

"So this is where he lived."

"I figured we'd start with the old man's bedroom," Jake said. "I'd like you to check around and see if you can find anything of value, antiques, stamps, old letters. Everything else you can put in one of those green garbage bags on the table. I gotta run out to the truck." He turned and lumbered back out the bedroom door.

It was difficult for Dave to imagine Old Man Henderson living here. The only place he'd ever seen him was when he was riding around town on that bicycle of his.

The room was cluttered with furniture, shelves and knick-knacks. Dave opened the drawer of a large desk and pulled out an ancient newspaper. It was dated June 12, 1956! Henderson would have been a young man back then, and maybe even normal.

A large, ancient typewriter sat on a corner of the desk. What would Old Man Henderson write on such a typewriter? Perhaps he was one of those cranks who was always writing letters to the local newspaper.

Dave sat down on the creaky folding chair, moved the typewriter aside, then carefully picked up a sheet of paper that had been wedged under it.

It was a poem! That was something he'd never have guessed! Dave looked at the bottom of the page for the poet's name. DBH. The "H" must stand for Henderson. He read the poem's title.

"I Love"

I Love? That was another surprise. He figured if Old Man Henderson was going to write a poem, it would be about grizzly bears or panning for gold up in the Yukon. He read on.

Dave looked up. He was shocked that Old Mr. Henderson could write such a poem…

Why do you think Dave thought that Henderson would probably write a poem about bears or panning for gold?

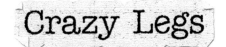

Crazy Legs

Crazy Legs! It just came to him. That's what Jerry and the other kids called Mr. Henderson! He felt a sense of shame wash over him. He returned to the poem. Who was Sonja? His wife? His sweetheart?

```
I love the feel of the wind on my face
The wide open countryside on the edge of town
The sun in my eyes
The exhilaration of the ride.

I love my bicycle.
When I'm on it I can forget.

I can forget the number
That's tattooed to my arm.
Forget the lost friends.
And almost . . .

I can forget Sonja.
When I ride my bicycle.
```

And what did he mean by "the number that's tattooed to my arm"?

Suddenly he heard the front door bang open. "Davy! You still here?" It was Uncle Jake. Dave stuffed the poem into his pocket and exited the little bedroom. "I'm up here, Jake." A large brown bag was tucked under Jake's arm. "Found anything valuable yet?"

"Uncle Jake," Dave said. "Did Old Mr. Henderson die? Is that why you were able to buy his house?"

Jake grinned again. "Nah. He had a mild stroke so they put his house up for sale and moved him into the old-age home." He studied his nephew's serious expression. "Why'd you ask?"

Dave shrugged. "Oh, I dunno." He paused. "Did you know that the old man wrote poetry? Or that he had a sweetheart named Sonja?"

The furrows on Jake's brow deepened. "Now how would I know that?" he asked. "All I knew about him was that he dressed funny and rode his bike around town. Everybody figured he was a bit loony."

Crazy Legs

"Maybe he was," Dave said. "But as soon as I finish here, I'm going to drop by the old-age home and pay him a visit." Dave hesitated for a moment. "I'd like to talk to him about riding bikes," he finally said.

"Bikes?"

"I was thinking about how Mr. Henderson loved riding his bike around town, and I remembered how great it felt to ride my bike when I was a little kid. Remember the feeling, Uncle Jake? When you're little, it feels like you're flying when you ride your bike fast – like you're a jet pilot or a racecar driver. I'll bet that's the way Mr. Henderson felt. Maybe that's why he whistled when he rode his bike."

Uncle Jake smiled at him. "Let me know what you find out, Davy."

Dave grinned, "I will, Uncle Jake. Now, let's see if we can find anything else of value in this old house."

People who are a bit different may be thought of as being a bit loony. What are some other different things a person might do that would cause others to think they're loony? How is this unfair?

Name: _____

Crazy Legs

1. What was Old Man Henderson known for?

2. What surprised Dave about the poem?
   _____
   _____
   _____
   _____

3. Why do you think Dave felt ashamed when he remembered that the other boys had called Mr. Henderson Crazy Legs?
   _____
   _____
   _____
   _____

4. Investigation: Mr. Henderson had a number tattooed on his arm. During World War II, several groups of people were tattooed in this manner by the Nazis. Name one of these groups.

5. Is it possible that in 1956 Mr. Henderson was as normal as the next guy? Give reasons for your answer.

6. Predict how Dave's visit with Mr. Henderson at the old age home will go. Describe what you think will happen during the visit.
   _____
   _____
   _____
   _____

Name: ——————————————

So That's Why They Call It
SAVAGE HILL

1. Every day we make decisions. Some may be positive, and some not so positive. Some are small and not that important, while others may affect the course of our lives.

   a) Give an example of a decision which might not be that important.

   b) Give an example of a decision which may have important consequences.

2. Some decisions are personal and might only affect you, while other decisions might change the lives of many people.

   a) Give an example of a truly personal decision.

   b) Give an example of a decision which would have consequences not only for yourself, but at least one other person.

3. The poet, John Donne, once wrote, "No man is an island."

   a) How might this quote apply to decision-making?

   b) Who in your life depends on you for making wise decisions?

So That's Why They Call It
SAVAGE HILL

I don't know what got into me the other day. Even my mom asked me afterward, "Whatever got into you, anyway, Craig?"

It happened last Saturday, and boy, what a fine winter's day it turned out to be. It was the week after Christmas and the snow had been coming down for three days straight! Joel Collins dropped by with his new GT Snow Racer – the one with three skis, steering wheel, raised seat – and boy, do they ever move!

"Come on, Craig," Joel said. "A bunch of us are going GT'ing on Beatrice Hill."

It didn't take much prompting for me to whip on my winter clothes and head outdoors, especially since I had just gotten my own GT for Christmas. But just as I was pulling on my ski pants my mom dropped a bombshell.

"Craig! I'd like you to take Shelby with you. He hasn't been outside all day."

What! Take my four-year-old brother out with the guys!

One look at my mother's face, though, told me that I would be wasting my breath complaining.

Shelby didn't have his own GT so I dragged my older brother, Ray's, out of the basement for him to use. Goodness knows where Ray was.

Joel was waiting patiently on the porch.

"Gotta take Shelby," I explained.

He looked at me from under his toque with that funny expression he wears when the old wheels are turning upstairs. So while we trudged down the street pulling our GTs, I waited for the bright idea I knew was coming.

I was right. About half way to Beatrice Hill he turned to me and said, "All the kids are over at Savage Hill this afternoon."

I stopped right in my tracks and looked at him, then at little Shelby struggling along behind us.

So That's Why They Call It
SAVAGE HILL

> If Craig does decide to go sliding on Savage, list one possible positive consequence, and one possible negative consequence.

"You know my folks won't let me slide down Savage when I've got Shelby with me."

"So. Who'll know?"

"Shelby will tell."

"Just tell him that if he squeals, you won't take him sliding with you again. Come on, Craig, Beatrice Hill is a complete waste of time. I can go down that molehill standing up on my GT."

"I know, but . . ."

"Yah, yah. Savage Hill is too steep, too many trees – but hey, with a GT you can weave in and out like you're driving a race car."

So that's how the conversation went, and before I knew it, there I was, standing on the top of Savage Hill. It was awesome! The hill was about two GTs wide, and as long as three or four schoolyards – and it wound in and out of about ten million spruce trees all the way to the bottom. And steep!

Joel was right – just about every kid in town was there that afternoon – bombing down, struggling back up, pulling their GTs and sleds. I tell you – it looked like they were having more fun than we'd ever have sledding down boring old Beatrice Hill, that's for sure.

Well, Shelby looked up at me with those big brown eyes of his, looking pretty scared, and for once he didn't want to go down by himself.

"Okay, hop on the back with me, Shelby," I said. "One of the other kids can drive your GT down for you." I looked over at Joel who was dragging his GT into position behind us.

"Make sure we have a good start before you go," I said. "I don't want you running us over."

So down we went. I couldn't believe how fast it was, and even though my GT could turn on a dime, I could barely manage some of those turns. And Shelby, who usually hoots and hollers all the way down Beatrice, was as quiet as a mouse, and I could feel his fingers digging into my sides – right through my parka!

Boy oh boy, did my mind ever start to work overtime during those few terrifying seconds that it took us to reach the bottom – especially since I was dumb enough to take my little brother with me!

> Why is it often foolish for a person to think he got away with something?

Finally, SWISH! we came out of the last turn and flew across the straight stretch at the bottom of the hill. We made it! For an instant I could hardly believe my good fortune, but there we were. Then something happened inside my head that I'll probably always be a little ashamed of. Right at that moment I was thinking, I did it. I got away with it. And I laughed to myself.

Shelby and I jumped off the GT and I lifted it up to bang the snow off the skis. For a few seconds I forgot all about my little brother, until suddenly I heard a yell behind me. Joel's GT was barreling down the hill, and right in his path was Shelby, running right up the hill, straight towards Joel. I'll tell you I've never been so scared in all my life. I thought my heart was going to stop beating right there and then. In that millisecond the thought went through my thick head, Shelby's going to be killed and it's all my fault!

Good old Joel though, I could have kissed him on both cheeks! He yanked that steering wheel at the last second – so hard that he went flying kit over caboose right past Shelby and into a clump of bushes beside the path.

Well, I don't need to be taught important lessons like that twice. I walked over and grabbed Shelby by the hand, and then we helped Joel out of the bushes.

"We're going over to Beatrice Hill," I informed them both.

Joel just banged the snow off himself and grinned. "Chicken!" he said.

I couldn't even think of anything to say back to him.

"Make sure Shelby doesn't say anything to your folks," Joel reminded me.

"He won't have to," I said. "I'm telling them myself."

Joel looked at me in that funny way of his, laughed and started back up Savage.

As boring as it sounds, I learned an important lesson on Savage Hill that day – how important it is to look after my little brother and set a good example for him. And you know, even though my folks weren't really pleased when I told them about our close call on Savage Hill, I think they gained a bit of respect for me because of my honesty – and that's important – even more important than the fantastic feeling you get flying down Savage Hill on a GT Snow Racer.

Name: _____

After Reading

So That's Why They Call It
SAVAGE HILL

1. How did Craig's younger brother complicate his plans about going sliding on his GT?

2. How did Joel further complicate things?

3. How was Savage a more exciting hill than Beatrice?

4. What do the names of the two hills seem to tell you about them?

5. Describe what must have been going through Shelby's mind as he went down the hill?

6. What happened at the end of the run that terrified Craig (and Shelby)?

7. What lesson did these events teach Craig?

Giving a Speech

1. Investigate: Research the names of two famous people (i.e. entertainers, politicians) who are deathly afraid of speaking or performing in public.

2. Why do you think public speaking is so frightening for so many people?

3. What do you think is the most important part of a speech? Why?

4. What advice would you give to a friend who had to give a speech, and was afraid?

5. Find each word listed in the WORD column in the article and examine its context. Define each word according to what you think each word means, then find out what the word really means from a dictionary.

WORD	GUESS	REAL MEANING
anxious		
caution		
rehearse		
confident		
strategy		
statistics		
hassle		
arouse		

A lthough it may seem hard to believe, many people are more afraid of giving a speech than they are afraid of snakes, spiders, heights, and even death.

Surveys reveal that 85% of people don't enjoy speaking before groups. Sweaty palms, rapid heartbeat, shortness of breath and dry mouth. Does that sound familiar? Even professional entertainers sometimes feel anxious in this situation. Some famous performers, like Kim Basinger and Donny Osmond, get very nervous before performances. If this is something that scares you, read on. Although there is no magic formula for curing stage fright, we may have some very useful tips to help you overcome this problem.

From what you already know about public speaking, what suggestions can you make to help someone who has a problem in this area?

The most important tip in helping a person feel more confident when public speaking is to make sure you know the material well. Speakers who don't take the time to prepare well enough, tend to be nervous, which leads to forgetfulness. Too often nervousness before giving a speech comes because the person doesn't know the material nearly as well as he/she should. Preparation involves learning about the topic, organizing your speech, making cue cards and an outline, and rehearsing (usually several times). This means practicing the speech until you know it well. Some people practice their speech in front of a mirror or onto a tape recorder or video camera. This gives them an idea of how they appear to others when giving their speech. If you feel comfortable practicing in front of a small audience (like your family or friends), this may also be a helpful warm-up for the real thing. Your practice audience might also be able to give you some helpful hints for improving your performance.

Giving a Speech

Writing the speech itself can also be very difficult. Sometimes the hardest part is actually choosing a topic.

When you choose a topic, always keep in mind who will be in the audience that you are speaking to. If you choose a topic that catches the interest of your listeners, then you have already reached first base. If you are giving a speech to your class, for instance, think of what might be of

Giving a Speech

interest to them. It should also be a topic you know fairly well. What do you talk about with your friends after school? What do you and your friends enjoy doing on the weekends? One word of caution – be careful you don't choose a topic that a number of other students in the class are already doing. Having your own unique topic is always a good idea.

> ## List three possible speech topics that would probably interest many students in your class.
>
> •
>
> •
>
> •

The introduction of the speech is the most important part. A startling statement, quote, or funny story can be good ways to begin a speech and catch everyone's attention. If you start your speech with a joke, make sure you can pull it off, because if your joke lays an egg, you may lose your audience. Also – if your only humorous material is in your introduction, your audience might feel disappointed when you remain serious for the remainder of the speech.

Don't pack your speech with too much information or you may bore your audience to tears. A way to avoid this is by giving illustrations, examples, or perhaps telling a short story to illustrate a point. Too many statistics can also put an audience to sleep very quickly. Personal stories can be an entertaining way of keeping the interest of your listeners.

Be sure to keep within the time limits of the speech. If the speech needs to be at least three minutes long, make sure your speech is at least 30 seconds longer than the minimum required. Most people speak faster when nervous, and tend to forget a point or two, which might drop you under the time limit. Going over time is a sure way to annoy the time keeper and bore your audience.

Giving a Speech

Although giving a speech in front of your class might seem like a real hassle, it allows you to practice a skill that you will probably need throughout your life. And like anything else, the more you practice it, the better you will get at doing it. One last suggestion: take seriously the ideas and feedback you receive from your teacher and friends. This will give you a good starting point at how to improve your next speech. Who knows? These skills might be the first building blocks in establishing a successful career in sales, acting, politics, or even . . . teaching!

As much as possible, look your audience in the eye. You can help yourself by writing key points or statements on cue cards. These points should be as brief as possible. This strategy will help you remember ideas, not words or phrases. Many who are new to public speaking try to cram as much information as possible onto the cue cards, which tends to make the speaker depend on the cards too much. Use a single word or two to suggest an idea, and keep each cue card to only three or four words. Finally, write these in large print so they can be read easily.

Remember to take it slow and easy. Speak the way you talk. Speed is not important in public speaking. In fact it can be a real problem. Natural pauses at the right times are also effective in pacing your speech and keeping your audience with you.

If it is possible that you are going to be giving your speech in a room that you aren't familiar with, try to go to the room a bit early so you can get used to the surroundings.

Your conclusion is also an important part of your speech. Try to end it with a bang. After summarizing your topic in a sentence or two, leave your audience something to think about, like a question or a challenge. This will be what they remember long after your speech is finished.

Name: _____

Giving a Speech

1. Complete the following chart. The column on the left describes different tips when giving a speech. In the right-hand column, explain why each tip might represent a danger.

TIP	DANGER
Start your speech with a joke.	
Don't put too much information in your speech.	
Pay attention to timing.	
Don't put too much information on each cue card.	

2. How can illustrations or props improve a speech?

3. How might the skills of giving a speech be useful later in life? Give an example.

4. Why is it important for a speech to have a good conclusion?

5. Why is it a good idea to listen to the suggestions and feedback received from people like your teacher and classmates after giving a speech?

Name: _____

1. Most people know that smoking can cause health problems. Give three more reasons why it is a bad habit.

2. Why do you think some teenagers start smoking? Try to think of at least two good reasons.

3. Do tobacco companies want young people to start smoking even though it is bad for them? If so, why?

4. Do you think seeing movie stars smoking encourages others to try it? Defend your answer.

_____

_____

_____

5. Choose a word that matches the meaning of the underlined word in the sentence.

The accountant worked in a tiny <u>cubicle</u>.

a) compartment b) apartment c) city d) circle

There are many hidden <u>perils</u> in a wild northern forest.

a) animals b) dangers c) trees d) insects

I don't want to find you <u>addicted</u> to the Internet.

a) attached b) working for c) dependent on d) not paying attention

Justin Forsyth trudged down the school hallway after his friend, Adrian Dumont. Adrian kept glancing back over his shoulder at Justin and raising his eyebrows knowingly. Something inside Justin made him feel uneasy about what was happening, but it was too late to back down now. Adrian led the way into the boys' washroom, and ordered a couple of grade five kids out. He beckoned Justin over to the far corner of the room and ducked behind a cubicle.

"What are you doing?" Justin asked, glancing back at the door.

"Take a look," Adrian said digging a pack of smokes from his pants' pocket.

SMOKING IN THE WASHROOM: A TRUE STORY

Justin glanced back at the door again. "You can't do that in here," he sputtered. "If you get caught they'll suspend the both of us."

"You worry too much," Adrian said pulling a smoke from the pack and then quickly lighting it. "Want one?"

> **Why do you think Adrian did this?**

"You know I don't smoke."

It was just like Adrian to show off like this, but this kind of stunt could really get them in a lot of hot water.

"Old Man Marsh is doing a lesson on the perils of smoking in health class next period," Adrian said. "I thought it would be neat to go to class with smoke on my breath. Know what I mean? Rub it in the old guy's big mustachioed face."

"We're going to be late," Justin said, turning toward the door.

Adrian took one last drag of the cigarette and flicked the butt into a nearby toilet. Justin scowled, then quickly ducked back into the cubicle and flushed the toilet.

When they arrived at Mr. Marsh's room, Adrian sauntered slowly past their teacher, who was sitting on a corner of his desk. "Hello, Mr. Marsh, Sir," Adrian said, putting his face real close to the teacher's as he passed.

SMOKING IN THE WASHROOM: A TRUE STORY

Mr. Marsh nodded a greeting to both boys. "Another ten seconds and you two would have been going down to the office for a late slip." He then turned to the class. "As I mentioned yesterday, we're going to be talking about smoking today. Any comments before we begin?"

Adrian winked in Justin's direction, then put up his hand. "You know, Mr. Marsh, a real good friend of mine started that nasty habit and I'm afraid he can't quit. I'm just so worried that he's addicted."

Mr. Marsh paused briefly. "Why do you call it a nasty habit, Adrian? What's so bad about smoking?"

Adrian grinned as several students turned in his direction. "Why, Mr. Marsh, I thought for sure you knew. It causes cancer, doesn't it?"

A couple of the kids snickered.

"Cancer?" Mr. Marsh echoed. He then turned to Sarah Bellefrey, who was definitely the cutest girl in the class – if not the whole school. "What do you think of smoking, Sarah?"

Sarah straightened in her seat and looked down at her pencil. "I think it is a bad habit."

"Why do you say that?" Mr. Marsh asked.

"My dad smokes and our house always stinks. I have to keep my bedroom door shut all the time or my clothes would smell. It also makes his breath bad and has turned his fingers yellow."

Janis Taylor, who was sitting across the aisle from Sarah nodded in agreement. "Yah, my mom smokes, and it's the same thing, only she has this real bad cough all the time, and the skin on her face is already starting to pucker and shrivel up like an old woman's – and she's not even forty yet."

"Does anyone else have anything to add?" Mr. Marsh asked.

No one said anything for a minute, and then Chuck Simpson, who sits right at the back of the room said. "My mom smokes too, and even though my dad's never smoked, he's had this real bad cough for almost a year now. We've been trying to get him to go to the doctor's, but he won't."

"Keep trying, Chuck," Mr. Marsh said. "Sounds like he's suffering the effects of breathing in second-hand smoke. That can be just as dangerous as smoking."

"That's what we tell him," Chuck said.

Mr. Marsh's gaze flickered past Adrian as he asked the next question. "Does anyone know what it costs to smoke a pack a day?"

A few of the kids made guesses, then Mr. Marsh said. "Go figure it out. How much is one pack? Now multiply that by 365."

There was a flurry of pens – then Dawson Floyd looked up and said – "Holy moly. I could buy a motorbike with that money."

"If smoking is bad for your health and costs so much, then why do people smoke?" Mr.

SMOKING IN THE WASHROOM: A TRUE STORY

> **Why do you think people smoke?**

Marsh asked.

"Cause it's cool," Adrian answered, the smirk back on his face.

"Why do some people think it's cool?"

"It just is," Adrian said. "Ever see that movie with John Travolta – I forget what it's called, but he looks so cool hanging out in that leather jacket with a smoke hanging out of his mouth."

"And James Dean," someone else chimed in.

"And Julia Roberts smokes . . . at least in her movies."

"Maybe it's because the tobacco companies are paying the movie makers to have the stars smoke," Mr. Marsh suggested. "Ever heard of product placement?"

"Yah," Chuck said. "That's where a company will pay to have their product appear in a movie or on TV."

"Sounds like a scam," Dawson said under his breath.

"What percentage of people in North America smoke?" Mr. Marsh asked.

"70 percent?" Sarah guessed.

"60?"

"Actually it's only about 30 percent," Mr. Marsh said. "So you see, most people really are getting the message – believe it or not."

Adrian grunted.

"And do you know that the vast majority of addicted smokers begin when they are about your age?"

"Well, I know a few kids who smoke," Sarah said, turning and looking directly at Adrian.

"It is a nasty habit, Mr. Marsh," Justin said. "I think we all know that. But what if someone smokes and really wants to stop? How can he stop?"

Mr. Marsh slid off the corner of the desk and walked up to the blackboard. "I'm glad you asked, Mr. Forsyth. Let's brainstorm some ideas that might be a help. He picked up a piece of chalk and turned to the class. "Well?"

Justin grinned as he watched Adrian open his notebook and take out a pen.

Name: _____

1. Choose two adjectives that would best describe Adrian's personality.

2. Why do you think Adrian challenged Mr. Marsh the way he did?

3. Why do you think Mr. Marsh often answered a student's question by asking another question instead of just telling them the facts?

4. What do the following terms mean:

a) secondhand smoke

b) product placement

5. Calculate. First find out the cost of a pack of cigarettes. Next, determine how much it costs a person to smoke a pack a day for one year, and for five years.

a) one year

b) five years

6. Mr. Marsh was going to brainstorm some ideas with his class regarding how to help someone who really wants to stop smoking. Come up with at least two ideas that could be included on his list.

Name: _____

SNOWBOARDING:
An Interview with Ingmar ("Ice Buster") Schtickler

1. What sport is similar to snowboarding? How are they similar? Different?

2. What athletic qualities do you think is important for a successful snowboarder to have? (Try to come up with two attributes.)

3. Investigate: name one geographical region in North America or Europe that would probably attract snowboarders for several months of the year.

4. **Draw a straight line to connect the vocabulary word to its definition.**

1. endurance
2. triceps
3. recommend
4. prefer
5. conditions
6. protective
7. extend
8. lunge
9. alpine
10. encase

a) to encourage something
b) mountainous
c) enclose
d) something that keeps you safe
e) the state of things
f) lurch
g) draw out; lengthen
h) like better
i) the power to withstand hardship or stress
j) an arm muscle

SNOWBOARDING:
An Interview with Ingmar ("Ice Buster") Schtickler

Q: Snowboarding is a very difficult sport. What do you think is the best way to get into it?

A: The quickest way to learn to snowboard is by taking lessons from a trained instructor who can teach you the basic skills that you will use for the rest of your riding life. Learning correctly from the start will keep you from forming bad habits.

Q: How important is it for a snowboarder to wear padding?

A: Falling is a part of snowboarding, and when you do fall, it can really hurt – sometimes even when you are wearing protection. Having padding protects your butt and knees. Wrist protection is another good idea, and a helmet. Serious injuries can result from hitting the back of your head on the hard snow.

Think of a question about snowboarding you would like to ask Ingmar.

Q: What are the main types of snowboards out there?

A: There are three main types of boards. The freestyle board is used mainly for jumps, tricks and halfpipe riding. The second type of board is the freeride snowboard. It is a solidly-built board used mainly for riding in open areas. The third type is the freecarve (or alpine) board, which is used for carving and racing. It is built for speed and is usually fairly long, stiff and narrow.

Q: Are there any important exercises that you would recommend for getting in shape for the snowboarding season?

A: A good upper and lower body workout can be very helpful. Aerobic exercises will also give you endurance on the slopes. Squats and lunges are excellent for strengthening your legs and the old stand-by, push-ups, are useful for building arm strength. A snowboarder can never have enough balance. Try placing a tennis ball under the ball of each foot, then do your best to balance only on the tennis balls.

Q: Can you tell me how important it is to wax your board before hitting the slopes?

A: Using the proper wax gives you the best possible ride. Believe it or not, each snow type and each temperature requires a special wax, otherwise your ride down the hill won't be nearly as exciting as it could be.

Q: At lunch I heard a couple of guys talking about skating on their boards. What on earth is that? I thought skating involves skates, not boards.

A: Skating is an important snowboarding skill. It actually refers to how snowboarders push themselves along with their back foot while their front foot is in the binding.

Q: Another term the guys mentioned was something I thought you only did on bikes. How on earth can a snowboarder do a wheelie?

A: A snowboard wheelie is actually balancing your weight on the tail of your snowboard while going down the slope. This means that the nose of your board will be off the ground and you'll be riding on just the tail. All you have to do to perform a wheelie is raise the nose off the ground by stiffening your front leg.

Q: What are the parts of the snowboard?

A: There are five main parts to the board. The nose is usually the end that points downhill, whereas

> **How do you think the sport of snowboarding might have gotten its start?**

the tail is the part that points uphill. The toe edge is the side of the board where your toes are. The heel edge, you guessed it, is the side of the board where you place your heels. Finally, the binding is the thing that binds your foot to the board.

Q: How long is a typical snowboard?

A: The length of a snowboard depends on how tall the boarder is. As a rule of thumb, a board standing on end should reach between the rider's shoulder and the bridge of his nose.

Q: My friend, Rob, took a pretty bad fall this morning and hurt his tailbone. Do you have any pointers about falling safely?

A: When you fall forward, be very careful of your fingers, wrists and elbows. A good idea when you fall forward is to make fists, bend your arms and hold them in front of your chest. Do your best to fall on your forearms, not your elbows. If you find yourself falling backward, tuck your chin into your chest, and twist yourself while falling so you land, not on your tailbone like Rob did, but on one butt cheek. A helmet will also go a long way to protect you!

Q: How did snowboarding get its start?

A: Snowboarding is a fairly new sport, invented in the 1960s. It began when an American named Sherman Poppen fixed two skis together for his daughter to surf down the hill near their home in Michigan. He called his new invention the Snurfer.

Name: _____

SNOWBOARDING:
An Interview with Ingmar ("Ice Buster") Schtickler

1. What padding is necessary when snowboarding? Why is this padding necessary?

2. Describe the purpose of each type of snowboard:

   a) freestyle

   b) freeride

   c) freecarve

3. Ingmar suggests a number of different exercises for snowboarders. Can you suggest another exercise that might be helpful?

4. Define the following snowboarding terms in your own words:

a) skating

b) wheelie

5. Describe the following parts of the snowboard:

   a) nose _____

   b) tail _____

   c) toe edge _____

   d) heel edge _____

   e) binding _____

6. Give one of the pointers suggested by Ingmar when falling from a snowboard.

Name: ——————————————————

THE HALLOWEEN SCROOGE

1. One of the characters in "The Halloween Scrooge" jumps to conclusions about someone else in the story. What does it mean to jump to conclusions?

2. Tell about a time when you or someone you know jumped to conclusions. What was the result?

3. When do people usually feel guilty about something?

4. What might a person do in order to stop feeling guilty?

5. Sometimes other people pressure us to do things we know are wrong. Why do you think we sometimes give in to this kind of pressure? What can be the result?

THE HALLOWEEN SCROOGE

Eric Jensen got up from the old wicker arm chair and walked to the edge of the porch. The cool autumn breeze felt good on his face as he gazed down the darkened street. Never could he remember a warmer, brighter Halloween night in all his thirteen years. Yet it still felt like he was sitting on pins and needles. Both of his parents had been called back to work after dinner, and his older sister, Shannon, was still out trick-or-treating with little Joey.

"Man oh man," groaned the other boy on the porch. "If this isn't the deadest Halloween of all time. Are hick towns always this dull?" His friend, Kyle, rummaged through the almost-empty bag of treats they had been passing out to trick-or-treaters.

Eric had thought it would be fun to invite his friend from the city to spend Halloween weekend with them, but things sure weren't working out as he'd hoped. "As soon as Shannon and Joey get back, we can take a walk around town and see what's happening," he suggested.

"Sure, but first maybe we can do something really exciting – like cut open Joey's apples and inspect them for worms, or count his bags of chips. Awesome!"

Eric turned away from his friend, his face burning. Ever since Kyle arrived this afternoon he'd been putting everything and everybody down, and Eric was quite sick of it.

"Look at the treats I got, Eric," Joey shouted, tripping over the last step. He opened his candy bag so Kyle and Eric could properly appreciate his triumph.

"Big deal," Kyle said with a sneer. "In the city we get twice that much."

Shannon moved up beside her brother, swinging back her long hair. "You have a lot more places to go than we do. We covered the entire town – every house."

"Yah," Joey piped up. "Even that old lady who just moved here, Eric. The one you

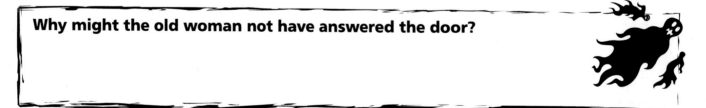

Why might the old woman not have answered the door?

THE HALLOWEEN SCROOGE

told us about on the edge of town."

"Did she give you anything?" Eric asked. Shannon tossed her head back again and reached for the screen door.

"Are you kidding? She wouldn't even come to the door. What a witch." She disappeared inside.

"Kyle and I are heading out now," Eric called after her. "You look after Joey." He bounced down the porch steps.

"Come on, Kyle."

"A witch," Kyle was muttering to himself. "A witch right here in this little hick town!"

"She's just an old lady that moved here a couple of weeks ago. I helped her put up her storm windows last Saturday."

"You gotta take me to her house," Kyle said.

It wasn't a long walk to the lonely cottage on the edge of town. Eric trudged the entire way, a worried look creasing his face. What was Kyle up to anyway?

"There it is," Eric said as they approached the dilapidated picket fence running around the house.

"What a dump," Kyle muttered. "If she ain't a witch, she sure oughta be."

"She's just poor."

"Come on," Kyle said. "Let's see if she's home." Kyle banged on the door and yelled. "Trick or treat!" Then he and Eric ran and hid behind a large bush by the steps.

There wasn't a sound from inside the cottage.

"Where's she keep her garbage cans?" Kyle asked.

Eric led him around to the back of the house. "She probably just went to bed."

Beside the back steps stood a dented garbage pail. "Happy Halloween, Witch!" Kyle lifted the lid and tipped the garbage can upside down, dumping its contents all over the steps. "Let's get out of here!"

Eric found it difficult to sleep that night and when he awoke the next morning he had a sinking feeling. Maybe the old woman didn't come to the door because she was sick or had a heart attack.

He was the last one up. Kyle, Shannon and Joey were already in the living room playing XBox.

"I'm gonna go check on something," Eric said, slipping on his shoes and jacket. "Tell Mom I'll have breakfast when I get back."

The cool morning air did a lot to clear the last of the cobwebs from his brain as he

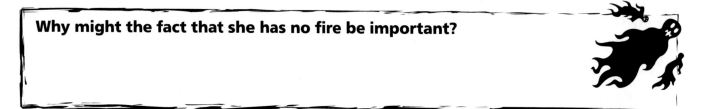

THE HALLOWEEN SCROOGE

jogged over to the old house.

No smoke from the chimney. Bad sign. He walked up to the front porch. "Hello!" He rapped briskly on the door. "Anybody home?" He heard a sound from the back of the

---

Why might the fact that she has no fire be important?

---

house. He sprinted down the steps and around the side of the building. At the back stoop, muttering softly to herself, an elderly, frail-looking woman was cleaning up the last of the garbage.

"Here let me help you," Eric said.

The old lady jumped at the sudden voice. "Goodness, you gave me quite a start, Eric," she said, straightening around to face him. She had a drawn, friendly face, and smiling hazel eyes.

"I'm sorry," Eric stammered. "I'm afraid a friend of mine did this, and it's partly my fault," he pointed to the garbage. "I'll help you clean it up."

"Ah well, that's nice of you." The old lady smiled. "Can't say I was surprised when I saw the mess. I didn't give out any treats last night, you know."

Eric knelt down by the steps and helped scoop up the last few bits of trash. "I noticed there was no smoke coming from your chimney."

"I've been so busy I just haven't had a chance to hire someone to bring me a load of firewood yet."

Eric paused, collecting his thoughts. "Listen, Ma'am, I was telling my folks about you moving into the neighborhood and my mother said that I should ask you over for dinner the next time I was talking to you. Would you be able to come over to our place for supper tonight? It would help make up for me being so dumb." He pointed to the garbage can.

"You are very thoughtful, Eric." She hesitated.

"Please," he said. "I have a friend staying with us for the weekend and I'm dying for him to meet you. It will do him a world of good."

The smile returned to her face.

"I'll pick you up at five-thirty then." Giving her a little wave, he trotted off toward home.

No firewood. No Halloween candy. Goodness knows how much food was in the house. She's definitely not a witch - just a nice old lady who needed help . . . and a friend.

Name: _____

THE HALLOWEEN SCROOGE

1. Why hadn't Eric enjoyed having Kyle over for the weekend?

2. Why did Shannon call the old woman who lived on the edge of town a witch?

3. Describe what the old woman's house looked like.

4. Because she didn't live in a nice house, Kyle thought the old woman was a _____.

5. Eric thought the old woman lived in a run-down house for a different reason than Kyle. What was it?

6. Why did Eric find it difficult to sleep that night?

7. Read the last paragraph again. What can Eric do to help this woman? (two suggestions)

The Boy in the Red Plaid Coat

1. Describe a time in your life when you were late for an important event. Make sure you describe your circumstances and your feelings at the time.

_____

_____

_____

_____

_____

_____

2. What is meant by a good Samaritan?

_____

3. Have you (or a friend) ever acted as a good Samaritan to someone? Describe what happened.

_____

_____

_____

_____

_____

4. Why is it sometimes surprising to be helped by someone you don't even know?

_____

_____

_____

_____

_____

5. Explain the meaning of the following proverb: Do unto others as you would have them do unto you.

The Boy in the Red Plaid Coat

"Hurry up, Frank. It's ten to eleven! We're going to be late!"

Frank bounded out the back door to the laneway where his mother was waiting in the family mini-van.

"You know how hard it rained last night," his mother said. "The back lane will be one big mud puddle."

"If I have a good practice this morning, Mom, I should make the football team," he said as they made their way down the laneway to the street.

Frank peered through the windshield at the mud-filled laneway, then glanced at his watch. He could forget about making the team if he was even one minute late. The coach was a real stickler for things like that. Good thing the field was only a few blocks away.

Why do you think the coach was so strict about being late for practice?

His mom leaned over the steering wheel, cautiously edging the van into the sloppy mess.

"Watch the spot this side of the sidewalk," Frank advised as they neared the street. "It looks pretty soupy."

His mother slowed to check traffic. Suddenly they were stopped, the back tires spinning in the mud.

"Back it up. Rock it, Mom."

"It won't move."

A feeling of panic swept over him.

What a time to get stuck. He scrambled out of the van. Thick mud oozed out around the back tires. Picking his way gingerly through the sloppy mess he leaned his shoulder against the middle of the back of the van, avoiding the worst of the spray from the spinning tires.

"Hit it, Mom!"

The tires whirled to life, spewing out a shower of muck, some sticking to his pants and overshoes. Again and again he heaved on the van. Reverse, then forward, then reverse again. So close – if only he had some help. He glanced again at his watch – ten fifty-five – they were going to be late! He looked up to see a small group of people passing on the sidewalk.

The Boy in the Red Plaid Coat

"Let's try it again, Mom."

The rear wheels spun obediently into action, but it was hopeless, What was even more discouraging was the people passing by didn't even seem to notice their predicament. A tall, dignified-looking man seemed to be leading the little procession past them. Frank recognized him from seeing his picture in the paper the odd time. He was some big shot down at city hall.

"Excuse me," Frank said.

The man turned in his direction. Frank pointed to the van beside them. "Would you mind giving us a hand? We're trying to get to football practice. I think one more person should be enough to get us on our way."

The smile disappeared from the man's face.

"I'd like to son, but I'm just not dressed for that sort of thing this morning." He gave an apologetic shrug, then continued on down the street.

Frank felt his face grow hot.

Several more people were approaching from the same direction. A middle-aged man in a long, beige trench coat glanced at Frank and the mired van.

"Excuse me, Sir," Frank said. "I wonder if you'd be able to give us a hand to push our van out onto the street?"

> Who do you think might stop to help Frank and his mom? Consider the person's age, sex, occupation, etc.

The man shook his head solemnly. "Sorry, but I've got a bad back. No more heavy work for me."

Frank turned helplessly to his mother. The procession of people had petered out – not that it really mattered. It was too late now, the practice would be underway in just a couple of minutes. His mother looked at him from the driver's seat. Frank could see the disappointment on her face. She knew how important making the team was to him and how hard he had worked for it. He could just see his brother, Kevin, laughing his head off when he heard what had happened.

Just then he heard footsteps behind him, this time from the opposite direction. The voice startled him.

"It looks like you need a tow truck."

A boy about his own age in a red, plaid coat stood before him, his hands thrust deeply into the pockets of his baggy pants.

Frank managed a weak grin.

"Doesn't look too bad," the boy said, doing a quick appraisal of the back wheels. "We should be able to get this out of here."

"You may get a little muddy," Frank smiled in spite of himself.

The boy in the red plaid coat grinned. "That's okay. I'm not exactly wearing my Sunday best."

The Boy in the Red Plaid Coat

Frank followed him to the back of the van and together they leaned their shoulders into it. Again the engine roared to life, tires spun, muscles strained, until finally the vehicle heaved itself free.

Frank and the other boy followed the van out onto the street and for a moment leaned, puffing against the back of the van.

His mother rolled down the window. "Thank you for your help."

The boy nodded politely.

"We'd better get going, Frank," she said. "We're late already."

"Thanks very much," Frank said, shaking the boy's hand. "Do you live around here? I don't remember seeing you before."

"I just moved in a few blocks from here." He nodded off to their right.

Frank hesitated for a moment by the passenger door. "We live in the big gray house half-way down the street. Why don't you drop by later today?"

The boy shrugged noncommittally. Reluctantly Frank crawled into the seat beside his mother. "Looks like I'm going to be late."

His mother glanced at her watch. "Looks that way. Maybe the coach will give you a break when you explain what happened."

"Maybe," Frank said. He thought again of the boy in the red plaid coat. "Whether I make the team or not, I'd like to get to know that guy who pushed us out of the mud. He seems real nice." Then he laughed. "You know what? I forgot to ask what his name was. Now I really do hope he drops in to see me."

After Reading
The Boy in the Red Plaid Coat

1. Describe the crisis that Frank encountered in the story.

2. How might Frank have avoided this crisis in the first place?

3. Why do you think Frank was especially disappointed by the first man's refusal to help?

4. How does Frank picture his brother reacting when he finds out about Frank's problem?

5. What does this tell you about Kevin's relationship with Frank?

6. Tell three things about the personality of the boy in the red plaid coat that you learned from this story.

Name: _____

Christmas with Aunt Libby

1. Many young people have mixed feelings about spending time with friends and relatives who are elderly (i.e., grandparents). List one thing that can be enjoyable about this experience.

2. List one thing about this experience which might be quite difficult for a young person.

3. Think of a time when you visited the home of an elderly person. Describe the experience. (Use as many of your senses as you can in your description.)

4. It has been said that during holidays such as Christmas, "it's more about giving than getting". What is your opinion about this thought? Explain your reason.

5. Investigate: Research one of the following people and explain why this person is remembered today.
   a) Florence Nightingale b) Terry Fox c) Mother Teresa d) Albert Schweitzer

Christmas with Aunt Libby

J eremy Wolfe slouched down into the car seat and stared gloomily out the window at the passing winter scene. Why did things never work out for him? Why, just once, couldn't his parents let him do what he wanted - especially at Christmas?

His mother turned and looked back at him from the front seat. "Aunt Libby is really looking forward to having us spend Christmas with her this year."

Why do you think Jeremy didn't want to visit Aunt Libby?

"I had plans," Jeremy said. "And as usual, they're ruined. Why can't we ever spend Christmas at home with my friends, instead of driving across town to visit our relatives."

"Since your grandmother died last year, Aunt Libby's been all by herself," his dad said.

"Her house smells like mothballs," Jeremy said, looking back out the window. "There's never anything to do." He knew that even though it was the day before Christmas, the next two days would drag by slower than molasses.

Aunt Libby lived in an old, two storey brick building on the edge of town. When she met them at the door, Jeremy was a bit surprised at how much older she looked than when he'd last seen her. She was still tall and stately-looking, though, with her gray hair done up in a bun. "Come in. Come in," she welcomed

with a wave of her hand. "Merry Christmas."

Jeremy gave Aunt Libby a half-hearted hug before being ushered into the chilly house. The family then gathered around the living room fireplace, close to the Christmas tree. Jeremy sank down onto the carpet in front of his parents, as close to the warmth of the flames as he could get.

"It is so good to have you all here for Christmas," Aunt Libby said. "I'm afraid it would have been pretty dismal spending the holiday by myself."

Jeremy's dad reached over and patted his aunt's wrinkled hand. "Spending Christmas with the family is what it's all about, isn't it?"

Aunt Libby turned to her great nephew. "You know, Jeremy, it seems like only yesterday that your dad was sitting right over where you are, waiting impatiently for Christmas morning."

"How long did you live with my dad and my grandparents?" he asked.

"Quite a few years," she said. "When your grandmother got so sick, I came to spend a few weeks to help out. Your grandfather was a salesman and traveled a lot, and your dad was still quite young. Then when your grandmother's health worsened, I decided to stay on. I got a part-time teaching job in town and helped out here as much as I could.

"Didn't you ever get married?" Jeremy asked.

Aunt Libby laughed. "No. I never did meet that special someone, and after awhile I just got too busy. I never regretted moving here, though, mainly because your grandmother was such a joy to be around – even with all of her pain."

"That sure must have interfered with your own life, though," Jeremy said.

"Perhaps it did, but I never thought of it that way. I had a very enjoyable career as a kindergarten teacher, and I found time to write poetry – even got a few published!"

"When Dad died, you really were indispensable," Jeremy's dad said.

"What was Grandma like when she was younger?" Jeremy asked. "I can only remember her when she was bed-ridden."

Aunt Libby smiled. "Your grandmother was a real practical joker, and she was also very athletic. She was such a good speed skater that she almost made the Olympic team." Her face suddenly became quite serious. "But I never heard her complain. For the last few years her arthritis was so bad that she could rarely even get out of bed. Even so, her neighbors called her Sunshine Granny, because she was always so cheerful."

"People visited her?" Jeremy's mom asked, surprised.

"Yes. Unfortunately as the years went by, fewer and fewer people dropped in. I guess everyone's so busy nowadays they tend to forget older people. I think toward the end of her life, she was actually quite lonely, though she never let on."

> **Why might old age be especially lonely for some people?**

"She was lonely?" Jeremy asked in surprise.

Aunt Libby nodded. "Old ladies get lonely like everyone else."

"It makes me wish we'd gotten over here more often," Jeremy's dad said sadly.

"You came by a lot, Bob," Aunt Libby said.

Jeremy pushed himself to his feet. "Do you mind if I see her room?"

"Of course not, Jeremy," Aunt Libby said. "I left everything pretty much the way it was when she was here."

"Do you want me to go with you?" his mother asked.

"It's alright. I'll be back in a few minutes."

Everything in his grandmother's bedroom looked exactly as he remembered it. The big double bed with the oak headboard, the tall mahogany dresser in the far corner and the large window overlooking the snow-filled backyard.

Above the bed hung a large picture of his grandparents, taken when they were first married. Jeremy stood, looking up into his grandmother's open, friendly smile. Her cheery

brown eyes were much like his own. A deep sadness suddenly swept over him as he considered how lonely it must have been – spending day after day shut up in this tiny bedroom. Why hadn't he visited her more often? She only lived across town… in fact his school wasn't even that far from here. He could have come over on his lunch breaks to spend time with her.

For some reason he suddenly found himself thinking of the old woman in the next room. Aunt Libby was almost as old as his grandmother – and now she lived here in this big old house all by herself! Were there times when his aunt was lonely too? At least his grandmother had Aunt Libby, but now Aunt Libby had only Jeremy and his parents.

His eye caught a picture of himself on the mahogany dresser. It was a school photograph taken a few years ago.

Jeremy sat down on a corner of the bed. He knew what he had to do. It may be too late for visiting his grandmother, but it was not too late for other things. He drew a deep breath and got to his feet. Being away from his friends for a couple of days didn't seem like such a big sacrifice anymore. More than anything, though, he just wanted to make sure that Aunt Libby was never as lonely as his grandmother had been. In the meantime, it was Christmas Eve – perhaps he could help make it one that his family would never forget – especially Aunt Libby!

Name: _____

Christmas with Aunt Libby

1. Why was Jeremy upset at the start of this story?

2. What two complaints did he have about Aunt Libby's place?

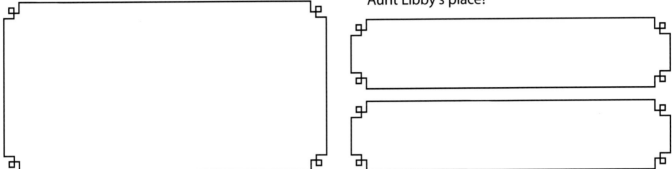

3. Jeremy's dad says, "Spending Christmas with the family is what it's all about". Do you think it is important for families to spend important holidays together? Explain your reasons.

4. How had Aunt Libby led a sacrificial life?

5. What did Aunt Libby say that saddened both Jeremy and his dad?

6. What resolution did Jeremy make at the conclusion of this story?

Name: _____

Before Reading

Airport Security

1. Why is airport security more necessary now than ever before?

2. What security methods would you recommend at every airport?

  •

  •

  •

3. Many people think having an armed Air Marshall aboard every passenger plane is necessary. Give one reason why this might be a good idea, and one reason why it might be a bad idea.

Good idea:

Bad idea:

4. Why do you think it is impossible to guarantee a plane's safety? Be specific.

5. Give one reason why terrorists now target airplanes.

T

he events of September 11, 2001 have changed the way people regard airport security the world over. How safe would you feel today if people were allowed to board a plane unchecked? What if no one checked to see if they were carrying a weapon or explosives?

Airport Security

At one time, though, it was possible to board an airplane with only the barest regard to security. It was also possible to board an airplane with items that are now banned. During the past twenty years, metal detectors and devices have been relied on at all major airports. These changes have been accepted by most people, because they know it makes them more secure. Most flyers feel that if a longer wait makes them safer, then they are willing to put up with it.

Increased security, though, has forced some drastic changes at airports. If you are going to fly in the near future, here are a few things that you can expect.

Why might some people complain about the increased security at airports?

Allow Extra Time

First of all, make sure you arrive at the airport in plenty of time. It is wise to contact the airline to find out how early you should arrive. Security people need time to screen all passengers as well as their baggage. In the past, terrorists have purchased tickets, packed their luggage with explosives, then sent the suitcase on board the plane without them. Now, no one may send luggage on a plane without boarding it. Allowing extra time is also wise during holidays, and other times when more people travel. If possible, take public transit to the airport, as parking and curbside access is limited. Many airports do not allow you to stop in front of the terminal to pick up or drop anyone off. These parking spaces are reserved for shuttle buses and taxis. If someone is dropping you off at the airport, make sure they park in the proper areas (even though this can be costly). If not, they may have their car towed.

Have ID Ready

Although it is not always required that a minor show his or her ID, it is a good idea to have these in order. Make sure you have two pieces of ID. One should be government-issued (e.g., birth certificate, health card). The other should include a photo. Not having the proper ID may result in a large hassle. You might even be stopped from boarding the airplane. Your ID and boarding pass may also be requested at several points of the check-in process. It is helpful to have a passport, although not strictly necessary within North America, though that rule may change. A passport is required when visiting most foreign countries.

Be Careful What You Pack

Once a passenger is checked in, only those with tickets are allowed beyond the screener checkpoints. Exceptions to this are small children and people with medical needs. At this point, each person is limited to one carry-on bag and one personal item, such as a briefcase. Everything else must be sent with the baggage. Electronic items, such as a laptop or cell phone, may have to undergo additional screening, like an X-ray. You will even find that your bags, including carry-ons and coats, are X-rayed and may be hand-searched. Don't forget to remove all

metal objects from your pockets before passing through the metal detectors. Don't carry anything that might be seen as a weapon (e.g., a knife, box-cutter, lighter, strike-anywhere matches, nail clippers with a file, scissors with pointed tips, etc.). Airlines can provide you with a more complete list of banned items.

Don't Let Others Use Your Bags

Always keep an eye on your bags when you are in the airport, and if you see an unattended package or bag, report it at once. Passengers not only have to worry about theft, but the danger of having unwanted items placed in their belongings (i.e., drugs, weapons, explosives). It may seem obvious, but never accept a package from someone you don't know. Be prepared to answer questions about who packed your bags and whether you might have left them unattended at any time. Think carefully about how you answer all questions. Criminals and terrorists have often used innocent passengers to board the plane with drugs or dangerous items. They do this by either tricking these passengers into carrying the item, or by slipping it into an unwatched bag. If you have any doubts about what your luggage might contain, say so.

What are some other items that airlines might possibly ban from flights?

Watch your Tongue

Never joke about having a gun or a bomb in your suitcase! Airport personnel are trained to react very strongly whenever they hear these words. You may think it is a joke, but it could mean going before a judge in a strange city. Every so often the media will feature a story about someone who joked about having a gun in their possession. Another way some people get into hot water is by over-reacting to a situation. This has come to be known as air rage.

How else might a passenger get him/herself into trouble?

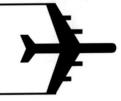

Airplane travel is still exciting, and one of the safest means of transportation. Although there is a lot of extra security nowadays that takes time, we can be thankful that the airlines are doing their best to keep our skies safe.

Name: _____

After Reading

Airport Security

1. From the information provided in this article, list three suggestions which make an airport experience more positive.

2. Why should you always keep your luggage in sight?

3. What might be the result of a passenger joking about having a gun?

4. Why do you think passengers are asked who packed their luggage?

5. If you were a security official at an airport, what are three things you would do to foil a terrorist?

6. Why do you think a photo ID is necessary for airplane security?

Name: _____

Before Reading

WORKING ON THE RAILWAY: MY FIRST SUMMER JOB

1. What would you like to do earn a living some day? Explain why.

2. What education is necessary for this job?

3. The main character in this story lived in northern Maine. Think about what this part of the United States is like and brainstorm with two or three classmates what possible summer jobs might be available in this region (three possibilities).

4. How might a summer job help prepare you for a full time career? Think about the work habits and skills you might acquire. Be specific.

5. What are some things you would like to have in a summer job?

-
-
-
-

My first summer job was not what most high school students experience. Our family lived in northern Maine, where mining and lumbering employed many local people. Summer jobs were rather scarce, so when I found out that the railway was hiring workers for their extra gang, I quickly signed on.

What do you think would be the ideal summer job for a student your age? Explain your reasons.

The extra gang was a crew of forty men hired to work on the railroad tracks deep in the wilderness. We slept in bunk cars parked along the siding on a remote stretch of track, ate in the dining car, and rain or shine worked eleven hours per day, six days a week, amongst a million tormenting mosquitoes and black flies.

The morning I arrived for my first day of work it was only 6:30 a.m., yet the men were already in the dining car having breakfast. I remember very vividly sitting down at the end of the long table and watching as thirty-nine men – all of them much older than me – wolfed down huge portions of ham and eggs, bacon, pork chops, baked potatoes, and a dozen other things that I might eat for supper. I looked at those around me in stunned silence. What a bunch of pigs, I thought, then poured myself a half bowl of corn flakes. Little did I know then, that by mid-morning I would be half-starved.

The work itself was really hard. Our job was to replace the old rotten railway ties with new ones. Each tie was about eight feet long, several inches thick, and seemed to weigh a ton. All of the old ties had to be removed from their place beneath the rails, and then the new ties had to be dragged under the rails and spiked into place. My first job was to take a shovel and deepen the trench where the new tie was to go. I quickly realized, however, that there was only one job worth having on the extras gang, and that was spiking the new ties into place. This job, though, was given to about a dozen of the strongest, most experienced workers, as it required a good deal of strength and skill. I quickly realized too that all of the men on the gang felt the same way I did – everyone wanted to be a spiker.

WORKING ON THE RAILWAY:
MY FIRST SUMMER JOB

As the summer days turned to weeks, I found myself dreaming about the day when I would be a spiker. More than anything, I wanted to bring that big hammer down on those spikes. Anything else seemed beneath me. I found it so frustrating that the foreman could not see how good a worker I was – how well I did my humble little job of trenching out the spot for the new ties.

My first step to reaching this goal came when one of the workers, whose job was to drag the wooden ties under the rails, became allergic to creosote – the black tar that coated all the new ties. It was then that I received the first promotion of my life – dragging the ties under the rails. Promotion! I can still remember the feeling of joy that flooded through me that morning, and how enthusiastically I heaved each of those heavy ties under the rails. A new guy was now trenching out the spots – for me! Surely now the foreman would recognize my talents and strengths and see how much potential I had for bigger and better things.

Why do you think it was so important for the writer that he be a spiker?

Yet two long weeks came and went before I was given another opportunity. By then I was probably the best tie-dragger on the railway. One rainy Monday morning one of the fellows didn't show up for work. His job was the second most important on the gang. He actually got to work alongside one of the spikers. With a long iron bar, he would pry up the end of the tie that was being spiked so that the wooden tie was flush with the bottom of the rail. Another promotion! Now I was only one short step from my goal, for I knew that the tie-holders were the ones the foreman always promoted to spikers. This was my chance. Never did they see a better tie-holder than I was that summer. I was always in there without ever having to be coached, always holding the tie firmly in place so that the spiker could sink his nails with as few swings as possible. I knew the routine. I'd watched the men a million times by now – always with an envious, watchful heart.

Finally – my big chance came. Unexpectedly, one of the spikers angered the foreman by breaking too many hammer handles and was quickly demoted to the back of the line – hauling water to the other men during break time. Immediately I was promoted from my job as tie-holder to spiker. I knew I couldn't get too excited. I had seen workers demoted and promoted before and it was often temporary. I knew it was a test. The foreman would be watching me – seeing how I would handle the responsibility for a few hours. How many hammer handles would I break? Would I take too long getting the spikes in – or tire too quickly?

I was almost desperate to succeed. There was just something glamorous about being a spiker – and I knew all the other men would have a new-found respect for me – especially the new guys. As I sweated under the hot sun, battling the blackflies and mosquitoes, I could just picture myself in the evenings back in the bunk car – the admiration showing in everyone's eyes when someone would tell one of the new guys that I was one of the spikers on the gang.

For the next three glorious days I was the happiest spiker in the whole of Maine. But alas, everything that I had hoped and dreamed of came crashing down all too soon. Before the end of the week we were told that our summer job in that part of the wilderness was complete and we were being released. No longer was I spiker on the extra gang. I was heart-broken. Back home I went – back to my parents, sister and friends. In only a few short weeks I'd be back at school. Even so, it was a very memorable first summer job. It is one that I can now look back to with a certain amount of pride. After all, it's not everyone that can say that he held the most important job on the railway.

Name: _____

WORKING ON THE **RAILWAY:**
MY FIRST SUMMER JOB

1. What summer job was the writer of this story able to find?

[ ]

2. List three things about this job that were difficult.

[ ]

[ ]

[ ]

3. Why was the narrator shocked at the breakfast eaten by the other workers? Why did this kind of breakfast turn out to be a good idea after all?

[ ]

4. The narrator of the story seems to be a person who values the prestige that comes with doing important jobs. Predict what kind of a job this person will end up with as an adult. Explain why you selected this occupation.

[ ]

5. Describe the four different job assignments the narrator had while working with the extra gang.

[ ]

[ ]

[ ]

[ ]

Name: _____

sex ed class

1. Why do you think so many students stress out when assigned an oral presentation in front of their class?

2. Why would doing a presentation on sex ed be even more difficult?

3. Is it important to cover sex ed in school as a part of the curriculum? Explain your response.

_____

_____

_____

_____

4. What are two topics you would recommend to be included in sex ed for grade 8 students?

5. Give one reason why it might be a good idea to separate the girls from the boys for sex ed classes.

6. Why do you think so many parents avoid talking to their children about sex ed topics?

Jesse Thompson sat at the table in the cafeteria sipping on a cola. Across from him slouched in his usual sloppy position was Karl Kennedy, eating from a bag of chips that looked as if it had been dug out of the garbage can.

"I've got no idea why you've worked yourself into such a sweat about this presentation, Jess," Karl said without taking his eyes off the half-empty bag of chips. "We took all this sex-ed stuff with Mr. McGregor a couple of years ago."

"I know, but my presentation is in front of the class, and that means the girls will be in there this time. What was Mr. McGregor thinking? They've always separated the boys and girls before for sex ed. Why did he decide to have us stay together for these stupid presentations?"

"What exactly are you nervous about?" Karl asked.

"Well, I did do the research on the two topics that Mr. McGregor asked me to, but it's just embarrassing to talk about stuff like that – especially in front of girls."

Karl nodded without saying anything.

Just then two girls from their class walked into the cafeteria and made straight for Jesse and Karl.

"Oh no," Jesse said with a groan. "Here comes Chelsea and Rachel."

Karl barely glanced up as the two girls sat down at the table. Chelsea beside Jesse, and Rachel beside Karl.

"All set for your presentation, Jesse?" Rachel asked.

Jesse tried his best at giving her as nonchalant a grin as possible. "Oh yah. That assignment was a piece of cake. I finished it up after dinner the other day." He looked over at Chelsea. "You're

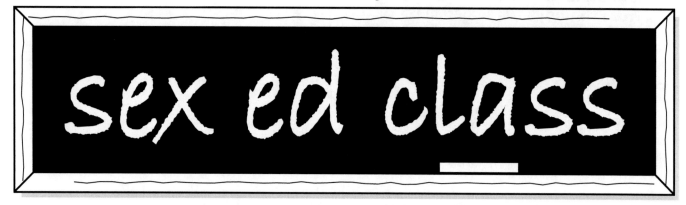

sex ed class

sex ed class

supposed to make a presentation in class today too, aren't you?"

She squirmed awkwardly in her seat, looking down at the folder in her hands.

"Yah."

"What's it on?" Karl asked.

"You know," Chelsea, said, her face turning a bit red. "You were there when he assigned the topics."

"I forget," Karl said.

"Well, then I'm not telling you," Chelsea said. "You'll have to find out in class."

"Oh come one, Chels," Rachel said. "Tell him."

Chelsea turned her head away from the others and watched as another student entered the cafeteria and bought a pop from one of the machines. "Why did Mr. McGregor have to assign these stupid topics, anyway? And why aren't we doing it in a separate class from you boys? That's just wrong!"

"Oh take it easy, Chels," Rachel said with a smile. "The topics are all on stuff we already know. All we have to do is go in there and do a two minute presentation on

it – that's all."

"Wait 'til it's your turn," Chelsea said. She turned to Jesse. "Aren't you nervous?"

Jesse shrugged. "I'm pretty good at giving speeches. I guess I'm a real ham at heart."

"He wants to be an actor and he figures this is good practice," Karl said.

	Why did Jesse act like the assignment wasn't bothering him?
○	

"Yah, but I mean, sex ed is kind of a yucky topic to be giving a speech on," Rachel said.

Karl laughed, finally looking up from his bag of chips. "Maybe I should get my dad to come and sit in on your talks this afternoon," he said. "He never explained anything to me. I remember asking him where I came from when I was about six years old, and he said, "from a turnip patch".

"A turnip patch?" Rachel echoed. "What does that have to do with anything?"

"My folks weren't much better," Jesse admitted. "I remember my parents sitting me down after we watched this embarrassing television program a couple of years ago, and my mom says, "Do you have any questions about the program that we just watched, Jesse?"

The girls laughed. "Well," Rachel asked. "Did you?"

Jesse grinned. "I made up some stupid question just to keep them from getting too excited."

"What about you two?" Karl asked. "Were your parents any better about talking to you about things like that?"

The girls looked at each other. "Not really," Rachel said. "Although my mom was pretty good about some things." She looked at Chelsea. "What about your mom?"

sex ed class

Chelsea shrugged and looked down at her folder again. "I actually had a long talk with my aunt a year or two ago. My mom's pretty hopeless about things like that."

"It is pretty important that we know certain things though," Karl said, "Otherwise we could end up in a dicey situation at some point. Who knows?"

"You'd think parents would take that sort of thing a bit more seriously," Rachel said. The others nodded.

"They probably find it pretty embarrassing and awkward," Jesse finally said.

"So what. It's our lives we're talking about here," Rachel said. "What with AIDS and all sorts of things going around, it's really important. I'm going to make sure I talk to my kids."

"We'll see," Karl said with a laugh.

"Anyway," Chelsea said. "Now I can sort of understand why it is important that Mr. McGregor go over this stuff with us. I mean our parents are all pretty good in most areas, but some of the kids in our class aren't so lucky."

"It's still a hard assignment," Chelsea objected.

"It is quite challenging," Jesse admitted.

The two girls looked at him in surprise.

"Really?" Chelsea said. "You're just not saying that?"

"No. It's hard to get up in front of the other kids and talk about something like this. It's kind of embarrassing."

○	Why do you think Jesse revealed his true feelings at this point?

"I know!" Chelsea said. "That's what I've been telling Rachel." She looked at Rachel with a frown. "Anyway, I do feel better knowing I'm not the only one who finds this assignment difficult."

"Say," Karl said suddenly. "You know what might help. What if we went down to Mr. McGregor's room right now and had you two practice your presentation in front of Rachel and I. We might be able to give you some pointers and it probably wouldn't be as tough when you do it later this afternoon."

Both Chelsea and Jesse paused as they considered their friend's suggestion.

"Actually, that might be alright," Jesse said. "I've kind of been wondering what the others will think about what I'm going to say. If I'm way off track, then you can let me know."

"Sure," Rachel agreed.

Chelsea got slowly to her feet. "Alright. Let's get this over with."

"Who knows," Rachel said with a laugh. Maybe Karl finally came up with a good idea."

"Now that would be a first," Jesse said, ducking as Karl took a punch at his arm.

"Come on," Karl said, leading the way down the hall. "Let's get you guys prepared for the lion's den."

Name: _____

sex ed class

1. What was Jesse nervous about?

2. Why do you think Chelsea refused to tell the boys what her topic was?

3. Why did Karl suggest that it was important for parents to talk to their children about sex ed? Do you agree? Explain.

_____

_____

_____

_____

4. Explain briefly how the following students' parents dealt with sex ed.

Karl

Jesse

Rachel

Chelsea

5. What did Karl suggest they do in order for Jesse and Chelsea's presentation to be more effective?

Name: _____

1. Has there ever been a special place that you and your friends go?
   If so, describe this place and explain why it is special.

2. Think of a time when you visited a place for the first time. (Perhaps a strange town or city.)
   How did you feel? Why do you think you felt this way?

3. What does it mean when a person is "down on his luck"?

4. Think of two reasons why a person might end up in this state.

5. What help does society provide for people who are down on their luck?

The Bridge

There's a bridge not far from our apartment building where my friend, Jon, and I like to go in the summer. It's a great place to have fun – like catch fish or skip stones in the river. Mostly, though, it's just a great place to hang out. And even though we live in a pretty big city, the river water is surprisingly clean.

During this past summer, though, we didn't get many chances to hang around there. Jon and I both got summer jobs down at the SuperMart, and so most days after work we just hung around the apartment building, talking about what grade 8 would be like. Last Saturday, though, that all changed.

Neither of us had to work, so after lunch we got together in Jon's apartment. It was a real nice fall day, kind of windy and a bit cool, so after awhile we got into our jackets and decided to take a walk down to the bridge. It was getting close to lunchtime, so Jon made a few sandwiches and we grabbed a couple of sodas from the fridge.

The bridge was at the end of a quiet street so there was never much traffic there. It also had tons of room under it on both sides of the river. The river itself was narrow enough to throw a stone right across to the other side, and its bottom was real gravelly, so it was a great place to wade. Sometimes in the summer, Jon and I would just loll around in the grass by the river and talk for hours. It didn't even matter if it was raining, because the bridge made a nice cover over our heads.

As we approached the bridge that afternoon, though, we heard these voices coming from underneath it, and we smelled smoke from a fire. Jon and I were the only ones who ever came to the old bridge, so we didn't know quite what to do. At first we thought it was some other kids and

we were all set to tell them to get lost, but when we poked our heads under the bridge, there were these two people we'd never seen before – a man and a boy about our age.

"What the heck?" Jon says.

The two strangers heard Jon and looked up at us.

What do you think the two people are doing under the bridge?

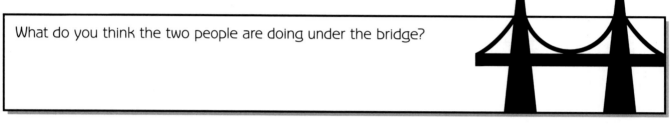

Jon whispers to me, "Let's see what they're up to." So we ducked under the bridge and slowly walked up to our two unwanted guests.

As we got closer we could see all these cardboard boxes, sleeping bags and other stuff lying around them. They actually looked like a couple of bums – the ragged way they were dressed and bundled up. In fact they looked like they were wearing every piece of clothing that they owned.

The man had been lying down beside the fire, holding a frying pan over the flames. He just looked at us but didn't try to get up. The boy, however, did. Not only did he get to his feet, I noticed he had a board in his hand, and he was just glaring at us. I then saw the older man reach up. "It's alright, son," he said.

The boy seemed to relax a bit.

"What do you want?" the boy asked.

"What are you doing here, anyway," Jon asked. "We're the only ones who ever come here."

"Haven't seen you here before and we've been here over a week," the boy said.

This guy had quite an attitude about him, and I could see that he really wanted to pick a fight with Jon and I. Only the older man was keeping him back.

"We come here all the time…" I said, but then stopped halfway through my sentence, because what the boy said suddenly hit me. If they had been here for a week, they must be living under the bridge!

"You boys are most welcome here," the man said in a raspy sort of voice. "There's lots of room for us all. We didn't mean to take your spot, but we're sort of in a pinch."

We moved closer to them.

"You're not from around here?" I asked.

"No," the man said with a faint smile. "My boy and I came to this city looking for work, but then I took a turn for the worse."

"Why don't you get an apartment?" Jon asked. "You can't stay here. It'll be snowing in a couple more weeks."

The Bridge

What solutions to their desperate situation might the man and his son consider?

The boy scowled. "Don't you think we haven't thought of that?" he said. "We spent everything we had on medicine for my dad. Not everybody has it as soft and cushy as some people."

I could see now how sick looking the man was. His face was pale and there were big dark circles around his eyes. "You'd better get to a doctor," I said.

"You need money for that," the boy snapped.

"Our family hardly ever has any money," Jon said. "My mom's out of work right now in fact, but when my little sister gets sick, my mom takes her to the clinic. It doesn't cost anything there."

"And you don't have to live here," I added. "There's a hostel not far from here that doesn't charge a cent to stay in, especially if you're feeling under the weather."

The boy glanced down at his father.

The older man cleared his throat. "We're pretty ignorant about city life," he said. "We're from a small town and when I got laid off from work we figured the best chance I had was in a city like this."

Jon sat down on the grass by the fire and opened up the sandwiches he had been holding. He handed one each to the man and his son and a half one to me. I could see the boy's eyes light up, but still he hesitated.

The boy's father, however, did not hesitate. "Thank you, lad," he said. "We've been eating rather poorly of late."

"Why don't you come along with us?" Jon said. "We've lived around here our whole lives. Once in a while our moms are laid off and money's scarce. We'll show you what to do and who to see."

The man looked up at his son again. "What do you think, son?" the man asked. I noticed the boy was now eating his sandwich and had laid the board back down on the grass.

The boy nodded his head. "Better there than being stuck under this bridge with winter coming."

"Come on then," I said. "We can all come back here in the summer – but it isn't all that great when it's twenty degrees below zero."

And so that was how Jon and I got to meet John Henry Pullman and his dad. Finding them under the bridge that Saturday afternoon was a bit of a shock, alright, but it sure gave me a much better appreciation for all the great things I have in my own life, especially that old bridge on the edge of town.

Name: _____

The Bridge

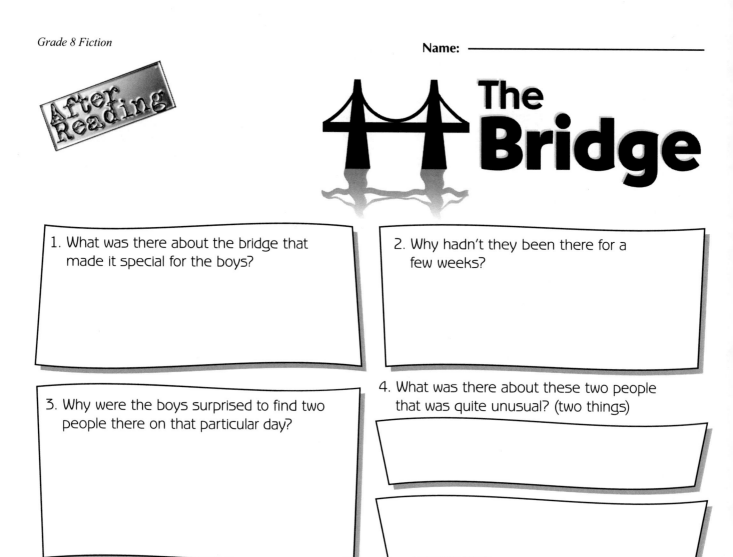

1. What was there about the bridge that made it special for the boys?

2. Why hadn't they been there for a few weeks?

3. Why were the boys surprised to find two people there on that particular day?

4. What was there about these two people that was quite unusual? (two things)

5. Describe the new boy's attitude when they first met him.

6. Why do you think he acted this way?

7. How had the man and his son ended up under the bridge in a strange city?

8. How did the boys think they could help the man and his son?

DEFIANCE PEAK

1. Describe a time in your life when you formed a first impression of someone.

_____

_____

_____

2. In the case you described, was your first impression accurate? Explain.

_____

_____

_____

3. How do you think a smart aleck would act when you are meeting him for the first time? (Be sure to give details.)

_____

_____

_____

_____

4. Why might a smart aleck behave this way? (Give two possible reasons.)

_____

_____

5. Why do you think it is usually more difficult to keep a secret than blab the information to someone?

_____

_____

_____

6. Define phobia and give an example.

_____

7. Do you have any phobias?

DEFIANCE PEAK

I never liked Clarence Woolings – not from the very first day I met him. He struck me as one of those smart alecks who thinks he's better than everybody else.

One Friday night not long after Clarence moved here, a bunch of us decided to hike up Defiance Peak.

"We'll meet outside the Jiffy Mart at 8:30 tomorrow morning," Jack, our unofficial leader said.

But wouldn't you know it – just as I was leaving the house the next morning, my dad gets me to move this humongous dresser out to the garage. So, of course, I was late.

When I finally did get to the Jiffy Mart, who should be sitting on the steps but Clarence. He was new in town and had been hanging out with the guys for a week or two. I grimaced as Clarence climbed to his feet and sized me up. He was a bit shorter than me but looked like he could handle himself in a fight. His hair was really short, so short it was hard to tell what color it was, and he had this long square jaw, and pale, blue eyes that seemed to look right through you.

"Jack figured you were late and asked me to bring you along," Clarence said.

Bring me along! I must have turned six shades of purple, but managed to hold my tongue. "You didn't have to wait for me," I said. "I've been up Defiance Peak a dozen times."

Clarence just gave me his patented smirk and led the way to the trail leading to Defiance Peak.

Now I should tell you that Defiance Peak is only about 400 feet high. Although it's a pretty demanding hike, the trail up the east slope is really safe. The farthest you can fall is about ten feet. But once you get to the top it's a different matter. The summit is flat and craggy and the western slope is a steep cliff.

When we were half way to the mountain we came to a "Y" in the path, and I suddenly had an idea. I said, "I know a short cut to the top – if we take it, we can beat Jack and the others."

Clarence just shrugged and followed me off down the trail to the right.

As I mentioned, I'd been up the main trail to the top of Defiance Peak plenty of times – but the shorter route up the opposite side goes up this gargantuan cliff! Shorter, yes, but ten times more dangerous!

DEFIANCE PEAK

What about Clarence annoys the narrator of this story?

A few minutes later we were standing at the bottom of the cliff, looking up at the narrow footpath, which wound its way along the side of the rock face.

It really wasn't as bad as you might think. I'd been part way to the top last summer. It was scary, all right, but the path was wide enough to walk along, and there were quite a few trees and shrubs growing by the edge to serve as handholds and to help block the view below.

I didn't even bother to look back at Clarence as I started up the trail, but I couldn't help but smile. I'll bet muscle boy wasn't smirking now.

Upward I climbed, one hand on the rock face beside me, my eyes straight ahead.

Within fifteen minutes we were probably halfway to the top, making excellent time and I was still as cool as a cucumber – at least on the outside. I probably should have mentioned earlier that I have this thing about heights – they terrify the living daylights out of me! Never look down. I know that's the trick. If I looked off to my right I'd see nothing but wide open spaces and probably faint from fright.

Then it happened! One minute I was inching my way along the trail, one eye on the cliff beside me, the other on the footpath, when suddenly the trail just ended! Halfway up the mountain and we'd come to a dead end! I glanced back at Clarence – bad mistake! Far below us I could see the tops of the trees waving invitingly in the morning breeze. If I fell from here – I'd be killed – there was no doubt about it!

"What are you waiting for?" Clarence asked.

I glanced at him once again – this time keeping my eyes level so I wouldn't look down. "What do you mean?" Couldn't he see that the trail had ended? It was then I noticed just below the spot where the path ended, that a birch tree was growing straight out from the side of the cliff parallel to the rock face. One of the branches, in fact, hung right over the spot on the pathway that was missing.

"Don't you see?" Clarence asked. "The path continues on the other side of the tree – the gap's only a few feet wide."

I took a closer look and could see that Clarence was right. "How do we get over there?" I asked. "It's uphill and too far to jump."

"We swing over on the branch," Clarence said. With that he pushed past me. I flattened myself against the cliff while he moved to the edge of the pathway. Then, without even catching his breath he leapt, caught the

DEFIANCE PEAK

branch with both hands, and swung himself across the chasm to the other side.

My heart almost stopped! Clarence was safe on the other side, and I knew I didn't have enough nerve even to turn around and go back down the way we came. My poor old heart was beating so hard and fast, I was sure that Clarence could hear it. Somehow, I managed to force myself to calm down and think. The gap wasn't all that wide, and the branch looked strong and sturdy. Again my eyes drifted downward to the forest floor – far, far below…

"Come on," Clarence said. "You can do it!"

But I couldn't. I stood there trying to work up the nerve – willing myself forward… What was

> What was the narrator's main motivation for making the jump?

wrong with me? Clarence was going to see that I was a total wuss.

I could see him looking at me now – one hand outstretched toward me. That was kind of surprising. For once he didn't have that sneer on his face or his superior, holier-than-thou look.

Every muscle – every nerve - was just about as tense as they could possibly be… my heart was racing… my palms sweating… It's a wonder my knees weren't knocking together. Finally, though, I just did it. I steeled my mind, gritted my teeth, and sprang from the ledge toward the branch – arms outstretched. One minute I'm standing there, feeling like the biggest coward in the world, the next minute I'm sailing through the air – one hundred feet above the forest. Then – I felt my hands slam against the thick tree branch and I was swinging through space.

I would have been alright, too, if I'd just swung my body a bit more when I hit the branch, but I didn't, so when I landed on the ledge I immediately began toppling backward, my arms windmilling to keep from falling. Thank goodness for Clarence. As calm as anything he just reaches out, grabs the front of my shirt and yanks me forward! I made it! Clarence just stood there grinning - not his usual smirk, just a normal grin.

"Lot's of people don't like heights," was all he said.

Thinking back on that day, I realize how stupid I was to risk my life – and Clarence's – just to impress someone. But I also learned something else too. When we got to the top of the mountain I just knew that Clarence would tease me in front of the guys and tell them how he'd saved me from falling off the mountain.

But he never said a word. Not then – not ever. So I guess you can't always tell everything about someone by whether he smirks a lot, or lets on like he's Mr. Cool. Sometimes what's underneath can be a lot different. And that was sure true of Clarence – because since then I've come to know him a lot better – and I like him a lot more too – even though he still thinks he's Mr. Cool.

Name: _____

DEFIANCE PEAK

1. Why do you think the narrator decided to lead Clarence up the more dangerous trail to Defiance Peak?

2. What happened during their climb that stopped the boys in their tracks?

3. Describe what Clarence did to get by this obstacle.

4. What do you think finally motivated the narrator to jump?

5. What did Clarence do to save the day?

6. What happened when the boys met up with the others that surprised the narrator?

7. Do you think you would like Clarence? Why or why not?

Name: _____

Before Reading

MUTINY IN SPACE

1. Define: mutiny

---

3. Describe the kind of leader that would probably cause a mutiny.

2. Investigate: Where was it fairly common for mutinies to occur?

4. Imagine the circumstances where a mutiny might occur in space.

5. Name two of the Earth's important resources than may eventually be used up.

6. Do you think there are any planets in other solar systems that can support human life? Defend your answer.

MUTINY IN SPACE

Captain David Dray, United Nations Aeronautics, looked through the starboard porthole at the gray surface of the strange planet. Things were working exactly according to schedule – his schedule, that is. He laughed into his helmet's mouthpiece.

The speaker over his head crackled noisily. "This is IDA, Blue Bucket. Do you read?"

He adjusted the mouthpiece with his jaw. "This is Blue Bucket, come in IDA." He waited while his words were relayed back to Earth, several solar systems distant. IDA: International Data Assemblers – Space Branch, formed in 2026 for the exploration and development of habitable planets in other star systems, had sent Blue Bucket in search of uncharted planets.

The speaker crackled back to life, and the monotone of the earth-bound voice continued. "We feel that under the circumstances we have little choice but to accept your demands, Captain Dray. Let it be on record, though, that we deplore your actions. Your desertion of your comrades, Major Weston and Captain Forester, has shocked the world."

"At least I left them on a habitable planet. They'll be fine until you pick them up."

The sun of the nearby planet shone brightly through the capsule window. He looked again

Make a guess: why did Captain Dray abandon his comrades?

at the bleak horizon to his right. It was hard to believe that such a hot place supported life – it was so close to their sun. Yet it did – or so the most recent computer probe had informed him.

The overhead speaker once again broke into his thoughts.

"IDA advises you Captain, that the best time to make a soft landing on the planet is in twenty minutes. Remember that a mapping-surveying ship, such as the Blue Bucket, is not equipped with take-off gear. If, on the other hand, you agree to complete your mission and return to Earth, we will assure you . . ."

"Listen to me, you greedy parasites," he shouted into his microphone. "You think you can send me up here to take all the risks, while you take all the profits? You can get some other sucker to chart this planet for you. The computer has informed me that the air here is fit to breathe and that it is inhabited with human-like creatures. And as you know, there is iron ore by the ton here – iron that Earth needs so badly." He reached up and adjusted the

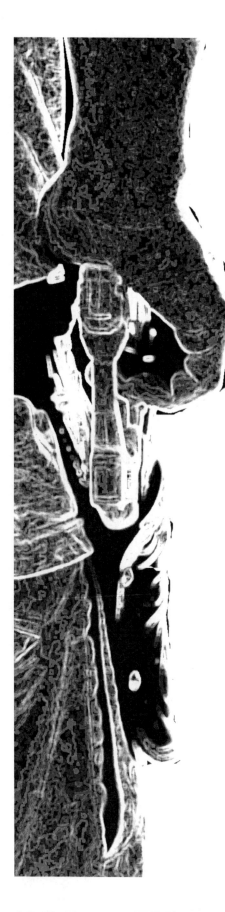

temperature control. It was getting increasingly difficult to control the heat this close to the sun.

"Let me repeat my demands, so that when the iron ore tankers arrive in seven months, there'll be no confusion. If you try anything funny, my laser guns have the power to knock your tankers out of the air before they land. I want five million dollars, guaranteed immunity and safe passage to the planet Ares."

Dray deftly moved the craft into its final orbit, and made preparations to land. He knew that the inhabitants wouldn't pose too much of a threat, no matter how advanced a civilization they boasted. His fingers traced over the butt of the laser-gun in his belt.

The controls operated smoothly beneath his skilled touch. He wished that the craft was still equipped for take-off, but the risk was worth the payoff. He just wished he didn't have to depend on the authorities back on Earth to get him safely out of here.

Seven months. Could be lonely up here. He checked his food supply – only enough for a few weeks – maybe a couple of months if he stretched things. Oh well . . . when the time came he would just have to eat what the natives did.

Less than a half-hour later the Blue Bucket touched down on the rugged terrain. Immediately, the sensors from the ship's exterior began taking atmospheric readings. Although very hot, 115 degrees, it was livable. The air was similar to oxygen, usable by the human body. With a deep breath, he stepped through the hatch. The heat struck him forcibly as he took his first steps on his new planet. It looked as though he had landed in the middle of the Sahara Desert! With a rising sense of panic, he hurried to the top of a nearby dune, sweating as he never had before. The heat was intense, yet the computer had said there was life on this planet . . . Where, then, were the people? All he could see was sand, and that blazing sun. He reached for his pocket transmitter. The computer in the Blue Bucket would be able to give him some answers. He punched his request into the mechanical brain.

The transmitter's sensors immediately began probing the horizons. Finally the tiny screen flickered to life.

LIFE APPROACHING FROM LEFT 300 METERS

Three hundred meters! He felt the butt of his laser, setting out cautiously in the direction indicated. The sand clung to his boots. Perhaps the particles were the iron he had come for. How sweet that would be. Perhaps the whole planet was one big ball of iron.

"Kretawni. Kretawni."

The shrill sound broke the stillness.

Jerking the laser gun from his belt, Dray instinctively dropped to a crouched position. A strange-looking, gray creature about his size stood on the hill and was pointing in his direction, or was it aiming a weapon at him! Dray whipped up his laser and fired.

What might be the consequence of Dray's action?

Emitting a sharp gasp, the creature toppled backward into the sand and lay still.

Fear gripped Dray. He hadn't really meant to shoot – it had all happened so fast!

Rising, he quickly brushed the sand from his clothing. He walked over to the fallen native, glancing around him as he went – searching the desert for additional creatures. He knelt down beside the fallen form, unmarked from the assault. Its eyes, arms and legs were similar to his, yet its facial features resembled some kind of nightmare. The head was very oblong, with no nose or mouth. In their place was a small hole at the base of its short neck. The voice must have originated from there. Where did it eat, if it had no mouth? The computer should know.

He moved the transmitter over the creature and turned on the built-in sensors, then waited for the miniature computer to spit out the required information.

Finally, the face of the tiny computer lit up. He began reading.

THE CREATURE IS COMPOSED OF ALIEN SUBSTANCES. ITS SURVIVAL DEPENDS ON THE EXTREME AND CONSTANT HEAT OF ITS SUN – SIMILAR TO A SOLAR PANEL. A MOUTH AND DIGESTIVE SYSTEM WOULD SERVE NO USEFUL PURPOSE, AS THIS PLANET DOES NOT SUPPORT ANY VEGETATION. FOOD AND WATER ARE UNNECESSARY FOR ITS SURVIVAL.

Dray sat down on the hot sand and picked up a handful of its round granular objects. He let them slip slowly through his fingers, then turned his eyes one last time up toward the hot, unblinking, killer sun, and shivered.

Name: _____

After Reading

MUTINY IN SPACE

1. For what reason was IDA formed?

2. What had Captain Dray done that had "shocked the world"?

3. What were Dray's three conditions to allowing the iron ore tankers from Earth to land on the planet he'd discovered?

4. What was the one snag in his plans?

5. Describe the circumstances in which Dray shot the creature.

6. Why was Dray doomed?

Name: _____

Let's Roll: The Story of Todd Beamer, Hero of 9/11

1. What two things about the 9/11 tragedy made the biggest impression on you?

2. Explain in your own words what you think a hero is? **3.** Name one person who you consider to be a hero. Explain why.

4. Explain in your own words what you think a coward is.

5. Describe a real or imagined circumstance in which a person might come across as a coward.

6. What is there in your life that you would be willing to stand up for?

7. State your opinion about this old saying, "He who turns and runs away, lives to fight another day". Do you agree or disagree with this saying? Explain why.

For too long our culture has said, "If it feels good, do it." Now America is embracing a new ethic and a new creed: "Let's roll." In the sacrifice of soldiers, the fierce brotherhood of firefighters, and the bravery and generosity of ordinary citizens, we have glimpsed what a new culture of responsibility could look like. We want to be a nation that serves goals larger than self. We've been offered a unique opportunity, and we must not let this moment pass.

- George W. Bush, State of the Union Address

Have you ever wondered what you would do in a situation of extreme danger, where your very life is on the line? What if an act of bravery saved the lives of those around you – your family or your friends or perhaps complete strangers? What if your actions could possibly cost you your life? A young man named Todd Beamer faced these very decisions one day not long ago, and his actions will be remembered for years to come.

Todd Beamer was a 32-year-old accounts manager living in Cranbury, New Jersey. Todd was the second of three children, raised in a home where faith was very important. In high school Todd enjoyed playing football, basketball,

Think of three words that would describe Todd Beamer.

On September 11, 2001 Todd boarded the doomed United Airlines Flight 93 to California. What was especially tragic was the fact that he normally would have taken the evening flight, but he had just returned from a holiday and was tired, so he took Flight 93 instead.

Shortly after take-off, four terrorists armed with box cutters gained access to the cockpit and took over the plane's

Let's Roll: The Story of Todd Beamer, Hero of 9/11

and baseball. After high school he attended Wheaton College in Illinois where he met his wife, Lisa. Todd and Lisa married after college and by September, 2001, had two sons, David and Drew. Lisa was expecting their third child.

"Todd could be a goofy guy," Lisa says. "He'd play with the kids, follow their lead. Drew was once walking around with a bucket on his head; he put it on Todd's head and Todd played along, bumping into things. He was very focused at work, but on a fun level he could roll around on the floor with a two year old."

controls. One of the hijackers said that he was carrying explosives and wouldn't hesitate to blow up the plane.

The passengers at first thought they were the victims of a routine hijacking. Some, however, had cell phones and were able to contact people on the ground, who told them about the two planes which had crashed into the World Trade Center in New York. They then realized that the hijackers probably planned to crash their plane in some dramatic way as well. By this time the cockpit door was closed and the 33 passengers and five flight attendants were being guarded by the hijackers who were not in the cockpit.

Let's Roll: The Story of Todd Beamer, Hero of 9/11

Like many of the passengers, Todd Beamer attempted to call home on his cell phone, but instead of getting his wife, Lisa, he was connected with Lisa Jefferson, a supervisor with GTE Customer Center in Illinois. Todd relayed to Mrs. Jefferson information about their situation, including the number of hijackers, the weapons they carried, and the number of passengers.

He then told her that he and several of the passengers, including Richard Guadagno, 38, Jeremy Glick, 31, and Thomas Burnett Jr., 38, were going to try to jump the hijackers.

"Are you sure that's what you want to do, Todd?" Mrs. Jefferson asked him.

"It's what we have to do," he answered. He and Mrs. Jefferson then recited The Lord's Prayer and Psalm 23 together.

Finally Todd uttered his famous words: "Are you ready, guys? Let's roll."

Honor Wainio, another passenger was on the line with her stepmother at this time. "I need to go," she said. "They're getting ready to break into the cockpit. I love you. Good bye."

"Everyone's running to first class," Sandy Bradshaw told her husband on her cell phone. "I've got to go. Bye."

"They're doing it! They're doing it!" screamed CeeCee Lyles to her husband on the other end of the phone line. Her husband, Lorne, then heard a scream and the line went dead.

What do you think happened at this point?

No one is exactly sure what happened next, but we do know from the cockpit voice recorder that Beamer and the other men fought with the hijackers. Shortly after, the plane crashed, killing all aboard.

It is believed that the hijackers were planning to crash the plane into either the White House or the Capitol Building in Washington D.C.

No one is sure exactly what happened to cause the plane to crash. Did one of the terrorists set off the bomb he was said he was carrying? Did the hijackers fly the plane into the ground when attacked by the passengers? Some even think that military fighter planes may have shot down the airplane to prevent it from crashing into another public landmark.

What we do know is Todd Beamer and the other brave heroes aboard Flight 93 gave their lives so that many more people might live. None of these passengers wanted to be aboard the plane when it was hijacked by terrorists, and none wanted to die on September 11, 2001, but they nevertheless put their own lives on the line to protect others.

Although it is possible that Todd actually said, "Roll it", instead of "let's roll", the term "let's roll" has become a catchphrase of freedom-loving people everywhere. President George W. Bush called it the new American creed in his State of the Union Address, and singer/songwriter Neil Young immortalized the words in his song by the same name.

Most of us hope that if we were ever faced with a life-threatening situation, we would respond as Todd and the other courageous passengers did, for in these men and women we have a wonderful example of modern day heroes.

Name: _____

Let's Roll: The Story of Todd Beamer, Hero of 9/11

1. Why was it ironic that Todd boarded this particular flight?

2. Describe how the hijackers gained control of Flight 93.

_____

_____

_____

_____

_____

_____

_____

_____

_____

3. How did the passengers aboard Flight 93 come to realize that this was not a normal hijacking?

4. What are three possible explanations for Flight 93 crashing when it did?

5. Why do you think Todd took the time to recite the two passages from the Bible before confronting the hijackers?

_____

_____

_____

_____

_____

_____

_____

6. Why do you think Todd's last words, "Let's Roll", captured the imagination of so many people?

Name: _____

Downloading Songs

1. How have computers and the Internet changed the way people access their music choices?

_____
_____
_____
_____
_____

2. What are two advantages in being able to download songs compared to buying them at a retail outlet.

3. Investigate: How has downloading music from the Internet upset the music industry?

_____
_____
_____
_____
_____
_____

4. What do you think about this?

5. Draw a straight line to connect the vocabulary word to its definition.

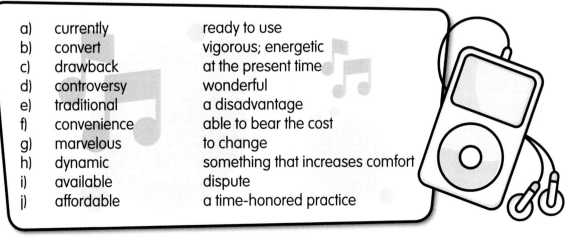

a)	currently	ready to use
b)	convert	vigorous; energetic
c)	drawback	at the present time
d)	controversy	wonderful
e)	traditional	a disadvantage
f)	convenience	able to bear the cost
g)	marvelous	to change
h)	dynamic	something that increases comfort
i)	available	dispute
j)	affordable	a time-honored practice

Many adults find it very difficult to understand just how far music technology has come in the last few years. To them it seems like only yesterday that they were listening to vinyl records on their mono "hi-fi", or popping a tape into their 8-track player.

Music has advanced through a number of interesting stages: from mono to stereo, to surround-sound; from record players to home entertainment centers; from eight-tracks to Walkmans to CDs to MP3s to… who knows where! Today's technology certainly has a number of listening advantages, and there are also factors of convenience. (It is hard for people to lug around a record player when they go out for a jog.) How did the marvelous MP3 invention come into being, and what exactly does it consist of?

Drawing on your own personal experience, name an important advantage to the MP3 format.

The development of the MP3 started in Germany back before you were born in 1987. It was first known by the name of EUREKA project EU147, Digital Audio Broadcasting – quite a mouthful. No wonder the name MP3 is preferred today!

An invention that really helped the MP3 become successful was the creation of Winamp, a free MP3 music player. This application was created by two university students and is free to use. It wasn't long before other programmers created a whole toolset for MP3 junkies. New encoders (rippers) and decoders (players) were sprouting up every week. Search engines also made it even easier to find specific MP3 files, and portable players like the Rio let listeners take MP3 tracks with them wherever they go.

MP3 itself is not an illegal format, but offering copyrighted material for downloading is illegal, unless the original artist is being paid copyright fees. This is where the Napster site has caused so much controversy. When Napster hit the Internet in 1999, it allowed anyone with a connection to download almost any type of music they wanted. This was done by connecting them with other people's hard drives. Music recording companies view the MP3 as a huge piracy threat and have tried to shut down many MP3-related businesses. If everyone gets their music for free – who pays for the artists to make the music? Or the recording companies to produce the albums? There are, however, many MP3 sites which offer tracks from artists who have agreed to post their music for free. Other sites sell MP3 files from established bands (both albums and single tracks).

Downloading Songs

The name MP3 is short for MPEG, which stands for Motion Pictures Expert Group which was a committee involved in the development of this form of technology. Simply put, the MP3 actually shrinks the sound data from a CD to one-twelfth its size, without losing sound quality. This means that the listener can hold many more songs on an MP3 player than on a CD. An MP3 player converts MP3 files back to standard audio format and then sends them to the computer's sound card, which in turn outputs them to the speakers or headphones.

Since the beginning of 1999 the popularity of MP3 format has exploded, so that major manufacturers have flooded the market with portable MP3 players. Music sites are also springing up everywhere on the Internet, offering free MP3 music as well as music to purchase.

Downloading Songs

One of the reasons why the MP3 is so popular is that it makes it very easy for people to mix and match their favorite songs or bands. For instance, if you want to make a "tape" of all your Beatle songs, all you have to do is search through your music folder on your computer, put the songs you want on a playlist and then send them to a CD burner for recording. Once mega-MP3 portables are available and affordable, you'll be able to take hundreds of hours of music wherever you go.

Another rising area for MP3 technology is webcasting, or streaming audio, where MP3 files are broadcast like traditional radio.

Why might it be an advantage to be able to record from a cassette or minidisk recorder?

A major drawback to the MP3 format is the fact that you may not be able to play the songs on your home stereo or in your car because standard CD decks won't recognize MP3s burned on a CD. In order to make this possible, an MP3 file needs to be converted to a wave (.wav) file first, then burned to a CD (which is a fairly easy process using a program such as Winamp). It is also possible to record your MP3 files directly from your sound card into a cassette or minidisk recorder. All that is needed is one-eighth-inch stereo miniplug cable from the output on the sound card to the recorder's input.

To create MP3s from your CD collection, you will need some "ripper" and "encoder" software. Encoder software takes the data from a CD and puts it on your hard drive as data. Remember that each song will take up about 40-50 MB of memory.

To turn the data into an MP3, you will need "encoder" software. Many of the free encoders have disappeared from the Internet, so all of the encoding applications require a small fee. Many of these programs will rip and encode as one process, so you don't need separate programs.

The most popular audio player is one designed by Apple Computer, called iPod. Most iPod models store media (music) on a built-in hard drive, although some of the smaller models use flash memory. A software program called iTunes is used for uploading music and photos. This is available to use on both the iPod and computer. This is like a music jukebox that organizes and stores music on the computer as well as playing and ripping it. The most recent iPod players are also capable of playing video. IPod was released in 2001 as a Mac-compatible product, but Apple later released a Windows version as well. Ipods can play MP3, wave files and many other files (including some games). Five generations of iPods now exist, including 1G, 2G, 3G, 4G and 5G. Apple sells two sizes of iPods: a 30 GB hard drive and a 60 GB model. Apple claims that one gigabyte of storage will hold 250 four-minute songs, so that a 30-gigabyte iPod can hold roughly 7,500 songs.

In the meantime, the MP3 format continues to become increasingly popular with no end in sight. The main reason for this is because it is just so easy to assemble a dynamite music collection which sounds great and can be organized to one's individual tastes.

Name: _____

Downloading Songs ♫

1. Name three stages in music technology.

2. List one advantage of the MP3 technology over:

a) vinyl records

b) CDs

3. The development of the MP3 started in the country of _____ in the year _____ .

4. What does the Winamp program do?

5. The article mentions one activity that is illegal. Describe what is involved in this illegal activity.

_____
_____
_____
_____
_____

6. Why is the MP3 format so popular?

_____
_____
_____
_____

7. Describe what the iPod player does.

_____
_____
_____
_____
_____

Name: _____

❊ METROPOLIS CITY NEWS ❊

Friday, December 27, 2004   Special Edition

TSUNAMI WREAKS HAVOC

Before Reading

1. What is a natural disaster?

2. Give three examples of a natural disaster.

3. Why do you think a natural disaster is sometimes referred to as "an act of God"?

4. A simile is a comparison if two things using the words like or as (e.g., "her city looked like a huge dumpster after the tsunami"). Use a simile to describe the aftermath of a car accident.

5. Circle the word that matches the meaning of the boxed word in each sentence.

The skiing trip into the mountains turned into a real |disaster|.

a) rally   b) triumph   c) tragedy   d) celebration

More than 400 people |perished| in the incident.

a) died   b) were injured   c) were misplaced   d) came together

The mysterious piece of |debris| from the barge was invaluable.

a) carriage   b) treasure   c) statue   d) junk

The table was |sturdily| built.

a) hurriedly   b) solidly   c) sloppily   d) shoddily

❦ METROPOLIS CITY NEWS ❦

Friday, December 27, 2004   Special Edition

TSUNAMI WREAKS HAVOC

Earthquake in Indian Ocean Triggers Devastating Tidal Waves

By John Smith

In the early morning of December 26, 2004, an earthquake off the coast of Indonesia set off a chain of events with devastating results.

The earthquake, located in the depths of the Indian Ocean, triggered a series of tidal waves, some reaching heights of 80 feet (25 meters).

The word tsunami is from the Japanese language meaning harbor wave. A tsunami can reach speeds of almost 500 miles per hour and can travel many miles before wreaking destruction. In 1960, an earthquake off the coast of South America started a tsunami that killed 150 people in Japan –10,000 miles away.

The Indonesian tsunami was responsible for the deaths of about 300,000 people. They were killed when the tidal waves swept inland on Indonesia and neighboring countries. Many of these people were tourists visiting from Canada and the United States. Although citizens from about 55 countries were killed, over 200,000 Indonesians are believed to have perished. The destruction is thought to have affected over five million people, with over a million left homeless.

The tsunami which happened off the coast of Indonesia was the worst ever recorded. It is

❧ METROPOLIS CITY NEWS ❧

Friday, December 27, 2004　　**TSUNAMI WREAKS HAVOC**　　Special Edition

uncommon for tsunamis to occur in this region, because earthquakes are quite rare in the Indian Ocean area. Only seven have been recorded in the past century. These monster waves are more common in the Pacific Ocean, where there were 17 tsunamis between the years 1992 and 1996, taking 1700 lives.

> **Why do you think it is so difficult to survive a tsunami?**

Most of the people caught in the Indonesian tsunami had little warning that disaster was close at hand. It was a beautiful, sunny day and the local people and thousands of tourists were enjoying the warm weather.

Tourists staying at a hotel in the country of Sri Lanka tell of watching from their second floor hotel room as a huge tidal wave came crashing ashore. It was so powerful that in seconds it reduced the first floor of the hotel to matchsticks. Some fortunate people were driven to safety on high ground before the next wave came crashing in.

One witness saw mothers with small babies trying to escape the wave, then saw the small babies being swept from their mothers' arms and washed out to sea.

Another witness from Europe told of being warned by the local people that a "killer wave" was sweeping in on the village. Although she escaped, her brother-in-law and parents were swallowed up by the wave. Her aunt ran to a nearby hotel but was submerged by the wave, which tore into the building. She was saved because she managed to grasp a table that was floating nearby.

Map showing countries directly affected by the 2004 Indian Ocean earthquake, which caused the deadliest tsunami in recorded history.

In nearby Thailand, tourists spoke of sunbathing and snorkelling, when suddenly they were warned by their guides that a "big wave" was coming. So they ran for their lives up the beach, barely managing to escape. They saw empty speedboats and fishing boats flying along the top of the water at incredible speeds, driven along by the fierce wave.

Many people, however, were not as fortunate. The local people living in the regions of devastation were especially hard hit. Many in these areas live in dwellings that are not sturdily built and unable to withstand a huge wall of water like a tsunami.

After the waves passed through, many areas were unbelievable sights. Dead bodies were everywhere. Experienced news reporters wept

❈ METROPOLIS CITY NEWS ❈

Friday, December 27, 2004   **TSUNAMI WREAKS HAVOC**   Special Edition

on camera as they described to their viewers what had happened. One reporter described her city as looking like a huge dumpster.

Many are saying that this natural disaster was the worst that has ever happened in the history of the world. Never before have so many people perished as a result of one natural event. We may never know the exact number of people killed.

Many of the world's countries, including the United States and Canada, rushed to the aid of the stricken nations. Food and emergency supplies were flown to the region as well as relief workers. Agencies like the Red Cross collected donations for relief. Musicians around the world planned concerts to raise money to help out.

Many of the countries devastated by the 2004 tsunami have come under severe criticism for not having a warning system for such an event. As a result governments are now working at putting into place a means of warning people of such an impending disaster. May we never again experience a tragedy of this magnitude.

How else might the people of these countries be helped to recover from this disaster?

Although it might seem unlikely that you will ever be caught in a tsunami, remember that many of the people killed in this disaster were foreign tourists. In case you are ever caught in the middle of such a disaster, here are a few things that might keep you alive:

1. Expect several waves. Many people were killed by returning to their bomes too soon – before the last wave had passed.

2. Head for high ground and stay there.

3. Don't worry about your belongings. You can always replace things, but you only have one life.

4. If you can't get to high ground, or you don't have time, go to an upper story of a sturdy building, or get on its roof.

5. As a last resort, climb a tree. At least a dozen people near Maullín, Chile, survived the 1960 tsunami by climbing trees. If you are swept up by a tsunami, grab onto something that floats – a tree, door, or a large piece of floating debris.

Grade 8 Nonfiction

Name: _____

❊ METROPOLIS CITY NEWS ❊

Friday, December 27, 2004   Special Edition

TSUNAMI WREAKS HAVOC

After Reading

Tsunamis are tremendously powerful.

1. Following a tsunami, ocean waves can reach a height of ☐ feet.

2. The waves of a tsunami can reach speeds of ☐ miles per hour.

3. Tidal waves from a tsunami have been known to have traveled ☐ miles.

4. The Indonesian tsunami killed about ☐ people and left ☐ homeless.

5. Tsunamis are relatively rare in the Indian Ocean. Only ☐ have been recorded in the last 100 years.

6. In the Pacific Ocean ☐ tsunamis occurred between 1992 and 1996.

7. One reporter described her city as looking like a huge ☐ .

8. Many believe the Indonesian tsunami was the worst natural disaster in the history of the ☐ .

9. If caught in a tsunami, you should realize that there will be several ☐ . To save yourself you should try to reach ☐ ground. As a last resort, climb a ☐ . If you are swept up by a tsunami, grab onto something that ☐ , like a ☐ .

10. Many of the countries hit by the tsunami are working on a ☐ system, in case such a disaster happens again.

Answer Key

Lost!: (page 8)
Before Reading: 1. Answers may vary. (e.g., take a compass; go with someone else) 2. Answers may vary. (e.g., wild animals; forest fires) 3. Answers may vary. (e.g., get a tracking dog or a human who is a good tracker) 4. Answers may vary. (e.g., a compass, matches in waterproof container, map) 5. a) tormentor; b) exhausted; c) prospector; d) overcast; e) landmark
During Reading: 1. Answers may vary. 2. Answers may vary. (e.g., climb a tree)
After Reading: 1. To cut some firewood. 2. It was overcast so he was unable to get his directions from the course of the sun.
3. To mark his trail so he might be followed. 4. Answers may vary. (e.g., panic; disorientation) 5. To escape the wolves.
6. Answers may vary. 7. He got Buster from Nelson Cheechoo to track Seth.

Crazy Legs: (page 13)
Before Reading: 1. Answers may vary. 2. Answers may vary. 3. Most older people don't ride around on bikes.
4. Answers may vary. 5. lumbered – sprinted; shame – honor; ancient – new; exhilaration – sadness; rickety – solid
During Reading: 1. Henderson did not appear to be a man who would write sensitive poems. 2. Answers may vary.
After Reading: 1. Riding around town on his bike. 2. The topic was "love" and the poem was quite sensitive. 3. Answers may vary. (Henderson now seemed more real to him.) 4. Answers may vary. (e.g., gypsies, Jews) 5. Answers may vary. 6. Answers may vary.

That's Why They Call it Savage Hill: (page 18)
Before Reading: 1. a) Answers may vary. (e.g., what breakfast cereal to eat) b) Answers may vary. (e.g., career choices, doing homework) 2. a) Answers may vary. b) Answers may vary. 3. a) Our decisions often affect others b) Answers may vary. (e.g., friends, parents, siblings)
During Reading: 1. Answers may vary. 2. The consequences may still be coming.
After Reading: 1. His mom made Craig take his brother with him when he went sliding. 2. Joel wanted them to go sliding on Savage Hill. 3. It was steeper and longer. 4. Answers may vary. (e.g., Beatrice sounds like the name of an old woman) 5. Answers may vary. (e.g., fear) 6. Joel and his GT were bearing down on Shelby who was in the middle of the trail. To avoid Shelby, he crashed his sled. 7. Answers may vary. (e.g., obedience)

Giving a Speech: (page 23)
Before Reading: 1. Answers may vary. 2. Answers may vary. (e.g., fear of failure; embarrassment) 3. Answers may vary.
4. Answers may vary. 5. anxious - nervous; caution - care; rehearse – practice; confident – sure of oneself; strategy – a plan; statistics – data; hassle – trouble or bother; arouse – awaken.
During Reading: 1. Answers may vary. 2. Answers may vary.
After Reading: 1. 1 – Make sure you can pull the joke off; 2 – It will make it difficult for your audience to follow and maintain interest; 3 – You will lose points for being too short or too long; 4 – It will make it difficult to follow the points. 2. It makes it more interesting.
3. It might help you to do well when performing in public in your chosen career, or in college. 4. It sums things up and is what the listeners remember. 5. They may give you ideas for improving your speech.

Smoking in the Washroom: (page 28)
Before Reading: 1. Answers may vary. (e.g., costly; dirty; stains clothing and fingers) 2. Answers may vary. (e.g., peer pressure; to look cool) 3. Answers may vary. 4. Answers may vary. (e.g., through attractive people smoking in ads and product placements in media) 5. a, b, c
During Reading: 1. Answers may vary. 2. Answers may vary
After Reading: 1. Answers may vary. (e.g., boastful; show-off) 2. Answers may vary. 3. To make them think for themselves.
4. a) non-smokers breathing in the smoke from other people's cigarettes. b) advertisers paying to have their products featured in the media (e.g., in movies and television) 5. Answers may vary depending on the local cost of cigarettes. 6. Answers may vary.

Snowboarding: (page 33)
Before Reading: 1. Answers may vary. (e.g., skateboarding, surfing) 2. Answers may vary. (e.g., balance, lower body strength, coordination) 3. Answers may vary. (e.g., Switzerland, Austria, British Columbia, Oregon) 4. 1–i; 2–j; 3-a; 4-h; 5-e; 6-d; 7-g; 8-f; 9-b; 10-c.
During Reading: 1. Answers may vary. 2. Answers may vary.
After Reading: 1. Padding should protect your head, bum and knees, and wrists. Padding is necessary to protect during a fall.
2. a) freestyle – for jumps, tricks and halfpipe riding; b) freeride – riding in open areas; c) freecarve – carving and racing.
3. Answers may vary. 4. a) skating: how snowboarders push themselves along with their back foot while their front foot is in the binding; b) wheelie: balancing your weight on the tail of a snowboard while going down a slope. 5. a) nose: the end that points downhill; b) tail: the part that points uphill; c) toe edge: the side of the board where your toes are; d) heel edge: the side of the board where you place your heels; e) binding: the thing that binds your foot to the board. 6. One of: bend your arms; hold arms in front of chest; fall on forearms; if falling backward, tuck your chin into your chest; twist yourself when falling to protect your tailbone; wear a helmet.

The Halloween Scrooge: (page 37)
Before Reading: 1. To form an opinion before learning all the facts. 2. Answers may vary. 3. When they feel that they have done something wrong. 4. Answers may vary. (e.g., make restitution) 5. Answers may vary.
During Reading: 1. Answers may vary. 2. Answers may vary. (e.g., she may be too poor to afford firewood)
After Reading: 1. Kyle was very negative. 2. The old woman didn't come to the door to give out candy. 3. Answers may vary. (e.g., it was old with a dilapidated picket fence running around it) 4. witch 5. She was poor. 6. Guilt. 7. Cut firewood for her; get her food.